CHESTER-LE-STREET

11. JAN 96

25 · 6 ·93

02. AUG 93
23. AUG 93

10. SEP 93
04. OCT 93
23. OCT 93
22. OCT 93

10. MAY 94

28. MAR 95

06. NOV
23. NOV 95
05. JAN 96

C713H25

No Easy Immortality

No Easy Immortality

J. H. REYNER

London
GEORGE ALLEN & UNWIN
Boston   Sydney

First published in 1979

GEORGE ALLEN & UNWIN LTD
40 Museum Street, London WC1A 1LU

British Library Cataloguing in Publication Data

Reyner, John Hereward
    No easy immortality
    1. Future life
    I. Title
    291.2'3   BL535   78–41235

    ISBN 0–04–200032–7

Typeset in 11 on 13 point Plantin by Trade Linotype, Birmingham
and printed in Great Britain by Cambridge University Press

Foreword

Although I had always had an innate belief in the survival of the spirit any speculation as to its nature appeared of purely academic interest. Death, I felt, would open the doors in its own good time.

I found plenty of interest in life and was even more fortunate in meeting Maurice Nicoll, who taught me how to try to live more consciously, as he himself had been shown by Gurdjieff and Ouspensky. There came a time, however, when I realised that this was not enough and that it is necessary to pay for one's experiences if they are to be significant.

This acknowledgement appeared to establish a communication with a superior level of intelligence from which a wide range of new ideas began to be received. In particular, I was shown that the hereafter of legend is not a mythical future state but is a realm to be inhabited at this very moment.

However, this cannot be done without appropriate payment. Hence it is both relevant and practical to try to discover the pattern of this real world so that one can learn to make proper use of its possibilities. To the extent that this can be done it seems that we make some small return for the privilege of existence.

J. H. REYNER

Contents

No Easy Immortality

1

The First Encounter

'What do you want to ask?' said my Angel one evening.

The question was unexpected, yet not to be ignored, for this was not the first time I had been spoken to by a voice beyond myself. The problem was how to answer it, for there are so many things one would like to know. Which will one choose?

However, it happened that I had been thinking recently about life after death, which was a subject on which I found conventional ideas far from satisfying. So I said, a little diffidently: 'According to legend, life is a continuing adventure and there seems to be clear evidence that the spirit survives the death of the body; but this adventure is usually deemed to relate only to some future state of existence. Are we not involved in it here and now?'

'Yes indeed,' came the reply. 'The spirit certainly has a continuing existence, but this is very much concerned with the present. If you knew what this involves you would understand many things which you find puzzling at the moment. But you must realise that there is no simple answer to this question because the conditions in the real world are directed by intelligences of a superior order which are unintelligible to conventional thinking. You have to stretch your mind beyond its habitual

1

limitations, and this is something you can learn; but tell me first why you want to know.'

'I suppose from a natural spirit of inquiry,' I replied, 'but recently I have begun to feel a certain sense of obligation. Life has provided me with a rich variety of experiences which I have, in the main, taken for granted. It occurs to me that these really ought to be paid for, though in what way I do not know.'

'Ah,' said my Angel, 'this is indeed important. Payment is a fundamental requirement throughout the Universe, in many ways and at many levels. Do you expect to attain understanding by mere wishing? This is a common illusion among mortals. Nothing of value is free, but if you can discover how to pay you will be given many things.'

'How then can I start?'

'You have already seen the answer, which is to cease to take everything as your right. Begin to ask yourself why you are provided with such a wealth of impressions from the world around you, and even more from the people in it. Why have you been given a body equipped with the intelligence which you take so much for granted?

'These things are not accidental, and if you will think about them more deeply you may find questions which I can answer; but only if you have taken the trouble to prepare the ground, because new ideas cannot be assimilated or understood unless there is something with which they can connect. So you yourself must make the first effort.'

The existence of angels is by no means generally accepted, let alone the possibility of conversing with them. The conventional mind, believing only the evidence of the senses, dismisses such ideas as fantasy. Yet it is known that the perceptions of the ordinary senses are severely limited, so that the familiar world is only a partial representation of reality. Ancient teaching affirms that man is a spiritual entity which is only inhabiting the physical environment for a brief spell. The purpose of the adventure is apt to be obscured by the excitements of life, but the spirit retains a tenuous contact with its origin which is represented in legend as a guardian angel.

One of the best known legends is Plato's Myth of Er,[19] a soldier who was slain on the field of battle and was placed with the other corpses on the funeral pyre. At the last moment it was discovered that he was still alive, and had a strange tale to tell. He described how during his few days of death he had been taken to the Bar of Judgement where he observed purified souls being allotted fresh lives according to their stature. They were then conducted by their guardian angel through the plains of Lethe, the land of oblivion, and thence down to earth to commence a fresh endeavour.

There are other legends which convey the further idea that the soul, bewildered by the events of life, forgets its purpose until it is reminded by its angel, which remains constantly in attendance to provide help when properly appealed to. This was indicated by the Stoic philosopher Epictetus, who said, 'God hath placed by the side of each man his own guardian spirit who is charged to watch over him – a guardian who sleepeth not, nor is deceived.'

The idea is not to be interpreted in terms of some mysterious protective agency which shields one from catastrophe. This is a popular but arrogant conceit which invests the individual with a wholly imaginary importance. There is a certain guidance in one's affairs beyond the personal contriving of the daily round, which Hamlet called 'the destiny that shapes our ends', but the principal function of the guardian angel is that of an intermediary through whom communication is possible with higher levels of consciousness.

Such communication is really wordless, using the language of ideas which is lighter and quicker than the ponderous processes of thought. This is the exercise of the emotional part of the mind which sees connections and relationships instantly; but because of the poverty of our ordinary understanding it is necessary to interpret the ideas in words, or as conversations.

The religions of the world are concerned with the establishment of contact with these higher levels of consciousness, which are usually represented as emanating from a personalised Supreme Deity to which various names are assigned. This appears to be the only way of conveying the sense of scale to the developing mind but the concept is easily contaminated with imagination and complacency. I found it impossible to envisage direct communication with this ineffable Intelligence and often felt the need for some intermediate and more practical contact.

One day when I was pondering this problem an inner voice said, 'Find the name of your Angel.' For a long time I did not know what this meant but I gradually became aware of a curious inner authority which seemed to accompany my daily activities, but not to be part of them, and I began to recognise this as the Angel I had been told to seek.

It did not appear in human form – of which indeed I would have been suspicious. There are people who are visited by spiritual messengers in dreams or trance states, but I am not a 'sensitive' and do not experience such imagery. Nor did I find it necessary to assign any name to this Presence. I was content to accept it as a superior Intelligence with which I was able to communicate if my mind was quiet.

The significant aspect of this communication, however, was that it did not take the form of lengthy and detailed disquisitions. I found that I had to make my own effort, by questioning my interpretation of many matters which I had complacently assumed that I had well understood. This created a more innocent atmosphere in which my Angel could talk to me when it was appropriate.

I realised that this was the beginning of the payment which was necessary for any real progress. We are familiar with the need for payment in material transactions, and psychologically we can appreciate that the attainment of any aim in life involves payment in terms of effort, which all too often we are not prepared to make. It does not seem to occur to us that our spiritual aspirations require a similar payment, and cannot be granted just for the asking.

It seems that one must start by questioning everything that one had previously taken for granted. This reawakens the sense of awe and wonder which we had as children but which we discard in the pursuit of supposedly more important things. Yet, as Thomas Traherne said in *Centuries of Meditations*, 'Is it not strange that an infant should be heir to the whole world and see those mysteries which the books of the learned never unfold?'

There is an Eastern aphorism which says 'That which a man has uncovered and explained, rightly or wrongly, he despises. That which he *discerns* – though its significance may be hidden from him – he bows down to and worships.'

2

The Unseen Pattern

An idea which I found acceptable from my youth was the premise that the world we live in is only a partial representation of a much greater but unmanifest reality. Superficially, it is not difficult to appreciate that things are not what they seem. Our awareness of the world is derived from information supplied by the senses, but these are strangely limited in their scope. For example, dogs can hear sounds which are inaudible to the human ear, a fact which is utilised in the 'silent' dog whistles sometimes used. Bats use even higher-pitched vibrations in a form of radar which enables them to 'see' in the dark, and there are many other vibrations to which the human ear does not respond.

Our eyes are even more limited in their perception, for science tells us that they only respond to a minute fraction of the total gamut of electromagnetic waves which permeate the surroundings, ranging from radio waves to the cosmic rays from outer space.[14] Perhaps the most dramatic implication of this limitation is that our very bodies, of such solid flesh and bone, exist only in our minds. They are really small enclosures of empty space populated by a vast number of almost infinitely small electrical charges assembled in such a manner as to appear solid to the perceptions of the senses. To a being with a different range of senses we would appear quite different – possibly we would even be invisible – and the same applies to the whole of the familiar world. I once asked my Angel why the senses should be so restricted. He said: 'Because if it were not so, you would go mad. Your brain could not cope with the vast influx of information. Every object in the physical world, whether animate or inanimate, is provided with a range of senses which is exactly sufficient for the fulfilment of its purpose.'

I found the idea that inanimate objects had senses strange until I realised that all natural laws are based on response to stimulus, so that everything must be equipped with some form of response mechanism. However, the reference to the purpose of everything suggested a further, more subtle reason to regard the familiar world as of only limited reality. We find from experience that its behaviour is very arbitrary. In some respects it is predictable, while in others it is governed entirely by chance, and although one adapts oneself to its vagaries it is sometimes difficult to discern any coherent meaning in the process.

The answer appears to be found in the idea that the phenomenal world – the world of appearances – is the implementation of a meaningful plan created by a higher order of intelligence. There are good grounds for this assumption. Science has discovered in the natural world such intricate and fascinating patterns of behaviour as to provide clear indications of conscious design. The eighteenth-century philosopher Immanuel Kant maintained that the events and objects of the phenomenal world were manifestations of energy which must *ab initio* be derived from a world of a superior order, which he called the *noumenal* world – the world of the mind.

This is a concept of great value because it conveys the idea of different orders of intelligence which appears to be essential for any real understanding. An analogy which I find helpful is that of a cinema performance. On the screen there appears a succession of situations and characters behaving apparently under their own control. Yet actually all these events are merely projections of images already recorded on a film produced by an independent mind and containing the complete history of the episodes which develop in sequence to the perceptions of the viewer.

On a much larger scale one can surmise that all the events and situations of everyday life are manifestations in passing time of an already existing pattern created by a superior intelligence in the noumenal world. The nature of this world will, of necessity, be only partly comprehensible to the ordinary mind, but it can be envisaged in simple terms as a realm containing a vast network of latent possibilities which are variously interpreted by appropriate senses.

The physical senses produce the appearances of the familiar environment but we possess a wide range of additional senses which respond to quite different influences. Some of these, often designated the paranormal senses, are responsible for supposedly supernatural effects such as clairvoyance and telephathy or the arts of psychometry and dowsing,[14] while there are others of a still more subtle character involving what are loosely called psychic phenomena. All these senses are part of the normal complement of human faculties though they are indifferently used. We do, however, respond to them occasionally by the exercise of what we call intuition.

Intuition is a faculty which is apt to be too lightly regarded and even suppressed. Yet it is really our most valuable asset, permitting the exploration of territories which are otherwise inaccessible. It has been defined as 'the immediate apprehension by the mind without reasoning', which is an excellent definition because it contains the implicit distinction between mind and intellect which is of vital importance.

The mind appears to be an instrument of much greater potentiality than is generally realised and as I began to think about it more deeply I was shown much more significant interpretations of its nature and function. Ordinarily it is loosely associated with thinking but it would seem that this is almost the

9

least of its functions. It is known, in fact, that all bodily reactions, whether physical, mental or emotional, are the result of incredibly rapid assessments by the brain of the information provided by the senses. But, wonderful as it is, the brain is no more than a mechanism and to perform its elaborate calculations it has to have been told how to interpret the information – in modern parlance, it has to be 'programmed' by some superior intelligence. This is the function of the mind, which is thus not part of the physical body but is a directing intelligence operating in the noumenal realm.

According to Gurdjieff the mind contains subdivisions, which he called Centres, responsible for the control of specific activities,[12] but in the present context the most important aspect of the mind is that it is extra-physical in character and thereby possesses extra-ordinary potentialities. Not the least of these arises from the fact that according to esoteric teaching the noumenal world is itself a structure containing a series of levels or storeys which are animated by progressively higher orders of intelligence, and the mind is similarly capable of operating at different levels. Its lowest level is concerned with the interpretation of the information provided by the physical senses, which forms the basis of all ordinary behaviour. By experience and habit this quickly becomes automatic, requiring no conscious direction. The higher levels of the mind, however, are designed to interpret the much more significant information from the noumenal world and thereby recognise relationships in the real pattern of existence; but these faculties are very little used in the turmoil of everyday life.

An important aspect of these relationships is that they are outside time as we know it. The varying events of life, which are perceived by the ordinary senses as separate in time and space, are really successive interpretations of an already existing pattern in the noumenal world, which the intuitive mind can perceive as a whole. This means that it can be aware of different parts of the pattern simultaneously and can communicate with people and events in different parts of space *and time*, since everything exists together in the noumenal pattern.

This is a startling idea to the conventional mind, but it is of the utmost significance since it changes the whole basis of one's understanding. The logical mind, conditioned by the sequence cause and effect in passing time, assesses all situations in terms of expectation. This quickly degenerates into imaginary and debilitating anxieties which bedevil one's existence. If this needless anxiety for the morrow can be set aside, as Christ enjoined so many years ago, it becomes possible to be increasingly aware of the underlying pattern existing in the real world. Events and situations are recognised as parts of a coherent whole and can be savoured quite differently.

Moreover, as the intuitive mind begins to function properly it can communicate with other people not physically present at the time, and can be aware of situations which have not yet developed, or are existing in other parts of the world. This is a familiar experience in dreams or conditions of trance when the normal consciousness is temporarily in abeyance, but it can be achieved by adepts during the ordinary waking state.

It will be clear that a consciousness of this order will not be restricted to the present but can operate within regions which are, for us, the past or the future. In particular, it will be able to communicate with people who are no longer inhabiting this part of time – i.e. the dead. This is an idea which the ordinary mind, so firmly conditioned by the sense of passing time, finds difficulty in accepting, and is often inclined to dismiss as morbid superstition. Others, perhaps still suffering the pangs of bereavement, embrace the possibility with foolish credulity. Both these extremes must be avoided if a true understanding is to be achieved, and I shall discuss later some of the many possible connections between the interwoven strands of the noumenal fabric. The concept, indeed, has a most inspiring quality because it confirms that we are not alone but are units in a vast and purposeful spiritual community.

I found the idea of the pattern in a noumenal world as containing the real cause of the events of life both acceptable and stimulating; but it remained an academic concept until I realised that I was not a mere onlooker, as is sometimes arrogantly suggested, but was myself part of the pattern, playing a virtually unconscious role in the sequence of events. It seemed important to seek a more conscious participation. According to esoteric teaching man has been created for this specific purpose, a special self-developing organism which by a certain kind of effort can achieve a spiritual evolution which legend represents as a return to the Source.

It is a progress in state rather than in time which has to start with the acceptance of the idea that the apparently haphazard situations of life are manifestations of an intelligent design. It is a design which, by its very nature, is beyond the comprehension of a mind conditioned entirely by the logic of the senses. The intuitive mind, however, can discern possibilities and relationships of a different order and this can create the beginning of an understanding of the real nature of the Universe.

I began to perceive that the journey had a certain impersonal quality concerned not with my own advancement but with the fulfilment of a plan which was both important and joyous. As was once said by A. R. Orage, a distinguished writer who studied under Gurdjieff at Fontainebleau, 'Everything we call natural is the product of beings superior to us, provided at great cost so that we may have the experience.'

It seems very ungracious to take it all for granted.

12

3

What is Life?

The idea that everything has to be paid for disturbs one's complacency in an unexpected way. I began to realise how deeply I was already in debt. The very ability to think on these things was a gift which I had never had the grace to acknowledge. Yet this was but a small part of the indebtedness. What of the astonishing profusion of impressions received by the senses every moment? Without these, existence would be meaningless, but we accept them as of right.

Do we realise the extent to which we are sustained by contact with other people, or feel any sense of gratitude for the wealth of meaning which we derive from their presence? All these opportunities are not accidental but are provided as part of the cosmic design. Man, however, is distinguished by the ability to use them consciously if he so chooses; but once he begins to do so he incurs an obligation which he can only attempt to repay by ceasing to take everything as his due. He is, in fact, living on credit and the debt which he seems to acknowledge least is that of life itself.

The earth on which we strut so blithely is covered by a curious film of apparently self-sustaining substance called organic life. It is almost negligible in thickness – of the order of one millionth of the earth's diameter – yet it includes the vast range of

13

organisms from microbes to animals, including man, which constitute the natural environment. What distinguishes this material from the inanimate matter on which it dwells, and is indeed itself composed?

The *Concise Oxford Dictionary* defines life as 'a state of ceaseless change and functional activity peculiar to organised matter'. This is an admirably succinct formulation of the behaviour of the phenomenon but it contains no clue as to what inspires the organisation. There are other definitions involving specific characteristics such as growth or ability to reproduce, but these again are descriptive of effects rather than causes. The constituents of living matter can be analysed, and even synthesised in the laboratory, but this will not create life. There is some additional factor, not expressible in physical terms, which directs the behaviour of living matter.

The world we live in appears in so many respects to be governed by mere chance that there are those who maintain that it is an entirely accidental structure which, like Topsy, 'just growed'. The film of organic life is assumed to be similarly accidental, having evolved from the primeval slime as a result of a chance concatenation of electrical discharges with certain hydrocarbon gases which produced the self-sustaining molecules of primitive life.

If so, there has been a remarkably intelligent direction of the subsequent development! The patterns of behaviour are so elegant that one must postulate the presence of a controlling intelligence of a superior order. It has always seemed to me that while the conventional theories of evolution may well be correct this could be the very mechanism which would be adopted by a superior intelligence as the most convenient way of implementing cosmic requirements.

I felt that in similar fashion life itself was an activity created by a higher level for some purpose which would not be apparent to the ordinary intellect and might indeed seem to be of no immediate concern. Yet, as Jerome K. Jerome said in one of his

14

essays, 'Life is to be lived, not spent', so that it seems right to want to know what one is involved in.

I found that, as had so often been the case, the clue lay in the recognition of different levels of manifestation and intelligence. The behaviour of the material world in general is determined by interchanges of physical energy of one form or another, energy which is harnessed in various ways, some natural, others by human contrivance; but no amount of this physical energy will create life, which is sustained by forces of a more subtle character.

Vital energy, in fact, is of a different order not compatible with material energy. Its real nature is a mystery. All one can say is that it is not part of the physical body, but only enlivens it for a limited period. We regard it as our most valued possession, whereas in reality it does not belong to us at all. As Death says to Everyman in the medieval morality play, 'Remember that your life is not your own; it is only lent to you.'

This mysterious energy is by no means an exclusively human property, but enlivens the whole of the natural world; moreover it is responsible for much more than the mere maintenance of life. The Polynesians call it *mana*, a property which is said to reside in all things to a greater or less degree and to give them their distinctive character. Some places have a peculiar concentration of this energy, resulting in an 'atmosphere' which we recognise intuitively without being able to say why; and we feel this even more strongly in the presence of certain people of unusual spiritual calibre.

The familiar world is indeed permeated by this intangible energy, of which we are vaguely aware as one of the conditions of existence. It does not occur to us to wonder why, and I said as much to my Angel.

'Try to think about how it is used,' he said, 'within the structure of an intelligent Universe.'

How then is this vital energy used? The obvious answer is that it serves to sustain the activities of the innumerable organisms which make up organic life. But these activities necessarily involve a continual dissipation of vital energy, which in an economical Universe cannot be regarded as inexhaustible. Hence there must be some provision for replenishment, for which purpose all living creatures are provided with the ability to extract nourishment from their environment. Every organism absorbs material food in some suitable form and converts it into the energy which it needs to perform its tasks. It is a familiar process, which we accept as one of the facts of life. Yet this activity is evidently not entirely physical since in the absence of the mysterious life force there is no action.

Something extra is involved here. Material food is a form of physical energy, whereas the maintenance of life is dependent on vital energy which is of a superior order. Nature therefore contrives what amounts to a continual miracle by equipping the organism with the ability to transform mechanical energy into vital energy. This is the process of digestion which is much more subtle than is normally recognised, involving a succession of transformations. The coarse material of the food is first refined in quality to allow it to be assimilated and used to reinforce the physical tissues; but this is followed by a still further distillation which creates the different kind of energy required by the vital level of the organism.[15]

This is a remarkable process which is exercised in appropriate form by all living creatures. It is an instinctive operation which does not have to be learned but is directed by the controlling intelligence of organic life, and serves to make good the energy which is dissipated by the various organisms in the discharge of their respective functions.

In the higher orders of life additional transformations can occur. The human body, in particular, is able to refine the vital energy into finer and more subtle forms required for the processes of thought and emotion. We take these activities for granted, without realising that they require energy for their operation. It is usually called psychic energy (using the word in its medical

16

rather than occult sense) and it is evidently of a much higher quality than that required for the mere maintenance of existence. It is in fact of a still higher order, not part of the structure of life itself.

A certain amount of this psychic energy is produced automatically in the body by the transformation of vital energy. This is arranged by the direction of cosmic intelligences which require human beings to be able to reason as part of the development of civilisation. However, this makes only a minimal use of the possibilities because man is equipped with an individual mind which can provide *conscious* transformations of the situations, if he so chooses. This is his real purpose, and if this facility is used it produces a range of psychic energies of a superior quality which have much greater potentialities.[12,15] They not only permit the exercise of the intuitive faculty mentioned in the previous chapter, but provide a certain kind of nourishment for the higher levels of the Universe.

Evidently there is here a pattern of remarkable intelligence. Yet this is only part of the story. We know by observation that the activity of any physical organism does not persist indefinitely. In due course the supply of vital energy is exhausted or cut off, and the organism dies. But every organism fulfils a certain function in the phenomenal world so that to preserve the necessary conditions there must be a continual supply of fresh material, which is provided by the natural processes of reproduction.

Now although we accept this as one of the conditions of existence it seemed to me that there was something significant in the idea that everything is fulfilling a purpose for a specified period. I put the idea aside to germinate, which in due time it did. Every organism, in fact, has a definite lifespan during which its quota of vital energy gradually becomes exhausted so that it has served its purpose and has to be replaced. In the cells of the human body this occurs roughly once a day while simpler organisms have even shorter lives. On the other hand, plants and animals which are assemblies of large numbers of cells have an identity which transcends the constant replacement of their constituent elements so that they have a more prolonged usefulness, usually measured in years; but they die in their turn when their vital energy is exhausted or is interrupted by accident.

Apart from this natural decay there is the continual slaughter of organisms for food. This is part of the established system wherein everything eats something lower in the order and is itself eaten by something higher. It is a process which is regulated by the controlling intelligence of organic life to preserve what is called the balance of Nature. For example, bacteria have an important function in the scheme of things; but they multiply so rapidly that if they were not preyed upon by phagocytes and similar organisms they would cover the face of the earth in a couple of days!

The balance may be disturbed by human interference or accidental changes of conditions but in the long term an appropriate harmony is maintained. Organic life, in fact, is a vast interwoven complex of death and replacement of which we are only fractionally aware.

There still remains the question of why organic life is necessary, and what purpose it fulfils in the overall pattern. It appears to constitute some kind of link between the physical and the noumenal worlds involving the transfer of energy in both directions. According to esoteric teaching the Universe is a system involving far more than the physical structure perceived by the senses. It can be envisaged as a hierarchy of intelligences originating from the Supreme Deity and becoming manifest in a succession of subordinate orders of increasing complexity.

Now, while these levels are distinct in quality they do not exist independently but are part of a coherent and mutually dependent structure.[12, 15] We exist physically in the phenomenal world, which is very low down in the order, but is still part of the pattern. It maintains its appointed role but is subservient to influences from superior levels to which it has not only to respond but has, in due course, to make an appropriate contribution.

Organic life is a medium provided for the reception of these extraterrestrial influences in the cosmic pattern. In physical terms it serves to collect and utilise radiations from the sun and planets which would otherwise be uselessly reflected (as they are from the moon). For example, the radiant heat from the sun is absorbed by the verdure of the trees and plants, but is then re-radiated in a slightly modified form which cannot escape from the earth's atmosphere, so that the heat is retained, producing the so-called greenhouse effect. At the same time the green pigment in leaves converts light waves into physical matter by the process of photosynthesis, and there are numerous other ways in which organic life adapts extraterrestrial radiations. Moreover, there are corresponding influences from the noumenal world which are similarly absorbed and utilised, though in a manner which is not detected by the ordinary senses.

I began to discern something of the pattern. Evidently the mass of living matter on the surface of the earth fulfils a cosmic requirement and is therefore arranged to be self-sustaining through the processes of eating and digestion; but these processes are so designed as to produce, as part of the operation, energies of a refined quality which nourish higher levels in the structure.

There is here again the implication of payment, but to appreciate this it seems necessary to consider more fully the idea of levels, which is discussed in the next chapter.

All this had a very impersonal aspect and I said as much to my Angel.

'What did you expect?' he replied. 'Individual significance? The Universe was not made for man, who is no more than a cell in the mind of God. But he has his place, as you will discover if you continue to stretch your mind beyond its habitual laziness.'

4

The Hierarchy of Levels

When I was a young man I knew well enough who I was – as we all do, for this is instilled into us at a very early age. I knew my capabilities and developed them with a satisfactory measure of success. However, at a certain time I chanced to meet the late Maurice Nicoll, who opened up for me entirely new horizons. (I know now that the meeting was not accidental but was contrived by my Angel, though at the time I was unaware of any such direction.)

Dr Nicoll was instructing a small group in the practical application of a system of psychology introduced by a Russian mystic, G. I. Gurdjieff, which is now well known.[12] Its basic tenet is that man is not fully conscious but is content with a purely perfunctory awareness, which is not even his own.

We customarily assume that our behaviour is directed by a mastermind which we call ourself. A more objective examination shows that in fact every situation is interpreted by an instantaneous (and unconscious) reference to a pattern of associations which has been built up in the memory by experience, and it is this which forms the basis of our judgements and actions – even our

21

thoughts. The trouble is that these reactions are by no means consistent. A slight change of circumstances can produce a different and even contradictory response.

It is as if the daily ritual were an unconscious drama performed by a variety of actors brought in on cue by the developing situations. Each in turn speaks its part, which is often necessarily in conflict with others in the cast. Yet with a curious perversity we identify ourselves with each of these fictitious characters as if they were real, saying 'I' to each and every one indiscriminately. Occasionally one of them behaves so outrageously that we are forced to wonder who is behind this façade, and we take refuge in an innate belief in some real but intangible entity which is (or should be) directing the performance.

Now according to esoteric teaching it is only this inner entity which is real. The 'person' in which we normally place the feeling of ourselves is no more than an automaton assembled by education and experience to contend with the requirements of life, which it does reasonably well, though by no means consistently. It is not even a unity, but a motley collection of characters which is not directed by any real consciousness but is entirely manipulated by the external influences of life.

Now to allow the feeling of oneself to reside entirely in this 'personality' is a fundamental sin – a word which means literally to miss the mark – because legend says that the whole object of the sojourn on earth is to achieve a growth of the spirit by making conscious use of the facilities available.

This is an idea of great depth which necessarily takes many years to assimilate, because one's belief in the imaginary self is so firmly established that one cannot accept the thought that one is not fully conscious. The first requirement would seem to be to understand what is meant by consciousness. It is conventionally assumed to imply being in full possession of one's faculties but the real meaning is far deeper. Literally the word means 'knowing all together', which is of much larger calibre. True overall awareness, in fact, must clearly exist at different levels not only in the physical world but still more in the noumenal realm.

Real consciousness thus has an impersonal quality, difficult to comprehend with the conventional mind, but it becomes at least partly intelligible within the concept of a hierarchy of levels of successively higher consciousness. The phenomenal world with its fascinating intricacies is not the pinnacle of the Universe. On the contrary it is, metaphorically, only the lowest slopes of the mountain. Beyond the perceptions of the senses is the vastly more comprehensive, but unmanifest, noumenal world which is itself a structure of levels, of increasingly refined quality.

This can be envisaged as emanating from the Absolute or Supreme Intelligence in a succession of stages subject to progressively increasing restrictions. Each stage will be enlivened by an appropriate consciousness, which will be fully aware of the structure and potentialities of its own level, and of all the inferior levels in the order, but will itself be subject to the direction of the superior levels. This means that the whole Universe is subservient to the will of the Absolute but in a manner which is determined by the level of the manifestation.[12, 15]

The totality of these levels is beyond man's comprehension but he has access to some of them. His body is subject to the laws and limitations of the phenomenal world but his spirit can operate in three further realms, which may be designated the Astral, Spiritual and Divine worlds respectively. They are regions of successively higher consciousness in which there is an additional dimension of understanding at each stage.

A higher level thus possesses potentialities which are not possible at a lower level. This may be illustrated by a simple analogy. A mite living within the surface of this page would be able to move in any direction over the area, but would be completely confined therein. It would have no awareness of the vast additional possibilities of movement in an entirely different direction out of the surface altogether. We have similar difficulty in envisaging the possibilities in a world of a higher order containing dimensions beyond those with which we are familiar.

Yet it is significant that even in everyday life we interpret the evidence of the senses beyond what they actually perceive. For example, our eyes do not register distance as such. It is inferred by reasoning. If an object such as a house, which we know from experience is quite large, appears to be very small we deduce that it is some distance away. There are certain primitive tribes which do not exercise this faculty. If they see a bird in the foreground looking larger than an elephant in the distance, they simply assume that they live in a world where some birds are larger than some elephants.

By the use of a suitably directed imagination we have developed the concept of the third dimension, which has become part and parcel of our life. In similar fashion we can, if we choose to make the effort, develop an understanding of the potentialities of higher worlds and begin to bring these also into everyday experience.

The first step is to think beyond the limitations of the habitual sense of time. Contrary to the usual belief this is not inborn but is acquired at a very early age because the senses, through which we relate ourselves to the external world, can only respond to *changes* of condition. Hence they are only aware of events in sequence, which creates the illusion of the passage of time. Yet the pattern remains. To take a very simple example, the words of this sentence are read by your eyes in succession, but the sentence is still in existence. It has not been destroyed by the movement of the eyes across the page.

Moreover, to continue the analogy, the meaning of the sentence is not contained in the individual words. It is only when these are interpreted as a whole that the meaning emerges. In similar fashion the events of life can be seen to be interpretations of an already existing pattern in the Astral world, which can be properly understood only at that level of intelligence.

This is the unseen pattern spoken of earlier, with the understanding that it is not a collection of events but of potentialities. The Astral realm, in fact, must be envisaged as a timeless region comprising a vast array of latent possibilities in which the interwoven patterns exist in (relative) perpetuity, so that it is, for us, eternal. Appropriate parts of these patterns are then interpreted in succession by the time-conscious intelligence of the phenomenal world, which thus presents events as isolated in time and space.

This is an intuitive concept, but we can understand the already existing nature of the pattern by analogy with a landscape through which we can travel in various ways. As we do so we encounter places and situations which come into being as we approach and disappear after we leave. Yet we know from experience that these places existed before we came and will continue after we have left (though with the march of time they may change their character).

In a similar manner the landscape of possibilities in the noumenal world exists in its entirety, but can only be recognised piecemeal by the ordinary senses which, as said, only respond to changes of condition. It is this which creates the illusion of passing time which so seriously hampers conventional understanding. A consciousness of a higher order will see the situations as a whole and will thereby possess a greatly expanded awareness.

It is important to realise that the hierarchy of levels is not merely an intellectual classification but is a living structure enlivened by a constant outflow of energy from the Supreme Intelligence. However, this energy is not dissipated endlessly. It has to be conserved by arranging that at each stage some mechanism exists for making good the wastage. The whole system is thus sustained by a rhythmical process of flow and return which is called in Hindu philosophy the Breath of Brahma.

Each level receives its quota of energy, suitably adapted to the particular conditions, which it utilises in the performance of its allotted functions. This involves the consumption of the materials of the environment but this is so arranged as to create energies of a refined quality by the mechanism of transformation mentioned in the previous chapter. In this context transformation is essentially a process involving a change of state and potentiality. A simple example is that of the metamorphosis of a caterpillar into a butterfly. Whereas the caterpillar lives in a virtually two-dimensional world on the surface of vegetation, the butterfly possesses an additional dimension of experience. Not only can it leave the ground and fly through the air but its life style is different. It feeds on different food and is itself eaten by creatures of a higher order – to wit, birds. It serves Nature in a wider way, being able for example to lay eggs (which, incidentally, hatch out as *caterpillars* so that the cycle has to be repeated).

There are many other transformations which occur in the natural world, one of the more spectacular being the development of a single fertilised cell into a child, which the eminent scientist Sir Charles Sherrington regarded as an occasion of great wonder. The cells do not multiply indiscriminately but at suitable stages they form specialist groups of structures and organs which are of higher intelligence than their constituent parts, culminating in a being of a different order, of use to a higher level of existence.

One can understand that at every stage in the hierarchy the activities of each level are so designed that as a kind of by-product they generate energies of a refined quality which nourish the level above and so replenish the system. It seems, moreover, that it is the residue of the transformations at any given level which provides the (suitably modified) energies for the succeeding stage.

We do not know the exact nature of these processes – nor need to because they are of cosmic dispensation, directed by the minds of the level concerned. However, there is one kind of transformation which we can understand, and have an obligation to attempt. This is the refinement of the energies of everyday life which results from the conscious participation in the events.

5

The Minds of the Universe

I found the concept of the hierarchy of levels inspiring, if only because it provides a practical expression of one's intuitive belief in the existence of superior orders of intelligence. Yet I was not clear as to the position of the phenomenal world in the scheme.

'Too big a question,' said my Angel, 'but I can give you a partial answer. You will appreciate that to permit the processes of replenishment which you have been considering there must be material available for transformation, and this has to be provided by each level of the hierarchy in order to sustain its own existence. Hence you can understand that part of the operation of the Astral consciousness is concerned with the creation and direction of the phenomenal world, from which it can then derive the nourishment it needs. Try to consider for yourself what this would entail, and how the intention could be implemented.'

Now this was a new idea which not only contained many possibilities but reinforced one's innate belief that the world did not come into being by accident, and I thought about it with delight. One can assume that the Astral consciousness will envisage in its entirety the design of a subordinate realm which will contain all the opportunities it requires. This will then have to be brought into being through the operation of a variety of directing intelligences or minds, each concerned with particular aspects of the creation.

In our conceit we regard the mind as an exclusively human attribute, which is absurd. There are many levels and qualities of consciousness, each of which employs a specific mind to interpret the available information; and this again is not confined to that supplied by the human senses. The behaviour of the whole phenomenal world, both organic and inorganic, is based on fascinating patterns of response to stimulus, directed by appropriate intelligences.

Hence one can see that there are several cosmic minds involved in the direction of the natural world. One is concerned with the physical structure, which is controlled by precise and elegantly formulated laws. Organic life incorporates the additional element of vital energy which is utilised within the structure by a number of subordinate intelligences concerned with the varied kingdoms and species (including the physical bodies of humanity);[14] and there are still higher qualities of mind, of a more individual character, which direct the operation of the functions of thought and feeling, together with, in man, the exercise of consciousness.

However, any intelligence requires a medium in which to operate. For example, the ideas which we try to convey to each other in speech are transmitted by vibrations in the (invisible) medium of the air. In the absence of air no sound can be heard. For the cosmic intelligences which direct the phenomenal world the necessary medium is provided by an intermediate structure, the non-physical and intangible medium mentioned earlier. It is sometimes called the etheric world – a term derived from the ether of the nineteenth-century scientists who felt the need for some extra-physical medium to conduct the vibrations which they were beginning to detect.

This etheric world may be regarded as the region containing

28

the underlying pattern of events – the 'blueprint' of the Astral design – and by this very fact it is outside the passing time of the senses. As previously stated, every object and event in the natural world can be regarded as the interpretation by time-conditioned senses of an already existing pattern in the etheric world; and this concept has an important implication, namely that the etheric world contains the long body or time-body of all earthly experiences. This is an idea which has been developed by various philosophers and it has for me a particular significance since one can see that the pattern will contain the time-bodies of many different people and events which will interact in a manner which will not be apparent at life level. The intuitive mind, in fact, can not only dwell in different parts of time and space but can be aware of relationships which are beyond ordinary perception.

In the case of living matter the etheric pattern has to accommodate an appropriate measure of vital energy. Dr Robert Crookhall, indeed, calls it the 'vehicle of vitality', which is an apt description of its function.[2] The vital energy is supplied by the Astral level and the etheric pattern is adapted to its use. When this energy is withdrawn (at death) the instructions are changed, being replaced by a programme of decay so that the material is re-used.

At first I was disturbed by the idea of the etheric pattern since it appeared to imply an irrevocable predestination, but I saw later that this was a wrong interpretation. The pattern can be modified by a consciousness of an appropriate order, which indeed we have to learn how to achieve; but if during the life there has been no more than a perfunctory awareness no modification is possible.

While I was thinking on these things I was shown a new idea of remarkable potentiality. It developed from the thought that every constituent of the material world has only a limited lifetime during which its energy gradually becomes exhausted so that it has to be replaced.

This is easy to understand in respect of the cells of the body, which are known to have a life of the order of a day or two; but what of the material of which these cells are composed? A cell is an agglomeration of chemical elements assembled in a particularly sophisticated manner of which science, by painstaking and inspired research, has discovered the pattern. These sub-microscopic atoms are beyond the perceptions of the senses. Their existence can only be deduced from observation of their behaviour, so that for most of us they do not have any real identity.

Yet there is an ancient Hermetic aphorism – as above, so below. Hence one can envisage that these invisible atoms are subject to the same laws as the much larger structures into which they are aggregated, which means that they will dissipate their quota of energy and will have to be replaced, but because of their vastly smaller scale their lifetime will be correspondingly shorter.

According to esoteric lore there is a factor of 30,000 connecting the time scales of the successive orders of manifestation.[12,15] If this factor is applied the lifetime of atoms is about 1/10,000 sec. This will apply to all atoms, which is certainly an unfamiliar idea. It means, for instance, that the material of this page will have been renewed many thousands of times while you have been reading it!

Yet these atoms are themselves composed of still smaller units – the electrons and other sub-atomic particles which science postulates as the ultimate constituents of matter, which by the same scaling down must have lifetimes so short as to have no meaning in normal terms; but curiously enough science does assign to these particles lifespans which are consistent with subdivisions by this magic factor of 30,000.

It is this progress to an apparent vanishing-point which provides the clue to the real situation, which is being approached from the wrong direction. The phenomenal world was not created by the Astral intelligence as a single act in some remote past but is a continuing process. Sub-atomic particles are assembled out of the void, to which they return when their energy is exhausted;

but because they are continuously replaced they acquire a corporate identity as constituents of atoms.

These in turn die but since they are constantly renewed their effective life is prolonged as the elements of material substances, including living tissues, and so on. One can envisage that the whole of the familiar world is literally coming into being at every moment. This is the real meaning of the word 'phenomenal', which is usually interpreted as 'displayed' (to the senses) but has a second and more significant meaning of 'coming into being', and I once in a flash of insight was aware of this happening before my very eyes. The static objects of the environment were quivering with motion.

This concept of continuous creation is of much deeper significance than is at first apparent. It provides an understanding of many so-called supernatural effects, because, if the visible world is continually being actualised out of the unseen pattern, an intelligence of a higher order can modify the instructions to produce phenomena which by ordinary standards are miraculous. Moreover, scientific thought today, in its quest for explanations beyond the perceptions of the senses, is beginning to formulate ideas which have a similar background.[14]

It is an aspect of the concept of recurrence which is discussed later. Both ideas can only be properly apprehended by the intuitive levels of the mind which respond to Astral intelligence, but they reinforce the vision of a living Universe which is continually coming into being at all its levels by the direction of the Absolute Creator.

6

The Place of Man

It is evident that the phenomenal world – the world of appearances – is a very limited portrayal of a structure of stupendous proportions and potentialities. Yet this is where we live, which would seem to indicate that man's potentialities are similarly limited.

'This is logical thinking,' said my Angel. 'In his physical manifestation man is no more than a highly developed animal, possessed of an intellect by the use of which he can achieve a measure of control over his environment. In cosmic terms this is of very small interest. Yet he has a special significance concerned with the development of his spiritual counterpart, for which the body is merely a temporary habitation. This is what you must think about.'

What then did I understand about this spiritual part? It is conventionally called the soul, though the word is interpreted differently in various philosophies. The *O.E.D.* defines it as 'the immaterial part of a man', but this is not entirely satisfactory because there are unmanifest aspects of phenomena which are still basically physical. I decided to regard it quite simply as the spiritual element in human beings, distinct from both body and intellect – a portion of the Divine spirit allocated to a man or woman for the fulfilment of a cosmic purpose.

33

What this purpose is may be obscure, but it seems certain that it will involve some individual responsibility. This is an idea which is apt to be ignored in conventional religions which assume that in the fulness of time the soul will automatically return to its Maker. I find this unacceptable for it entirely ignores the necessity for payment. It seems much more inspiring to believe that the return, whatever it may be, has to be paid for, and it is in discovering how to do this that the real adventure lies.

According to legend, the soul is created by the Divine level of the hierarchy, which is inspired by a consciousness incomparably greater than that which animates the phenomenal world; but it is deliberately created incomplete and has to acquire experience in all the inferior realms to complete its development. For this purpose it has first to descend to the level of earth to utilise the conditions which exist there. To the extent that it succeeds in doing so it is enabled to extend its experience into the Astral and later the Spiritual realms, and ultimately to become reunited with its origin.

Man thus does not belong to the phenomenal world, but only inhabits it. His physical body is created by the Astral intelligence and is directed by the impersonal minds of organic life mentioned earlier; but he is equipped in addition with an *individual* mind which is itself a multiple structure capable of operating at different levels. The lowest or formatory level is concerned with the establishment of satisfactory relationships to everyday events. It creates, by experience, a library of associations through which the information supplied by the senses is co-ordinated in meaningful form. This enables the individual to contend as best he (or she) can with the changing situations of life and many people are content with this mechanical existence, particularly if it provides success and comfort.

In this condition, which is called in the Gospels a state of sleep, man is no more than a superior kind of animal, making no use of the spiritual talents with which he has been invested. However, there are higher levels of the mind which operate within the Astral level of intelligence and if these can be used they create more conscious associations which respond to impressions from the unmanifest world. Events and situations begin to be interpreted as a whole, embracing not merely the physical manifestations but also the connections and relationships in the underlying patterns of the Astral world.

This heightened awareness transforms the quality of the experience and creates energies of a superior order. But this we have to develop for ourselves. It does not happen automatically, but exists as a possibility which the soul has to learn how to exercise by individual effort. The frustrations of life with its chequered pattern of pleasure and pain are really the raw material for these essential transformations, which is why the soul inhabits the phenomenal world, since it is only at this level that the necessary opportunities exist.

In these terms one can begin to apprehend something of the cosmic requirement. The transformation of the experiences of life produces a refined quality of energy which provides nourishment for the Astral level over and above that which is derived automatically from the long processes of cosmic evolution. This in turn permits similar transformations of energy at progressively higher levels, which invigorates the whole structure, and this is the purpose of man's creation.

At each stage an appropriate payment is demanded, and because of the enormous differences of quality in the hierarchy of levels this payment involves prodigious and sustained effort at each stage. As Virgil says in the Aeneid, 'Easy is the descent to Avernus; but to retrace one's steps and escape to the upper air – that is the toil, that is the labour.'

In practical terms this requires the awakening of the mind to its real potentialities; but this is not easy because the succession of events has a hypnotic effect which creates the illusion that life situations are sufficient in themselves, so that the soul forgets

35

its aim. Yet in a strange way it appears that this is necessary. As said earlier, according to Plato's Myth of Er the soul is required to drink of the waters of Lethe, the river of forgetfulness, before being escorted down to earth, so that it has only a faint memory of its purpose. It is said that more enlightened souls drink sparingly of these waters, but even so considerable individual effort is required to awaken from sleep, and it is this effort which constitutes the beginning of the payment which has to be made for spiritual progress.

One finds a similar idea in an early Christian poem of great beauty known as The Hymn of the Soul.[6] This dates from the second century AD and describes the adventures of a young prince who leaves the court of his father and descends into Egypt (representing the world of the flesh) in order to search for a pearl of great price which has been lost. To protect himself from the inhabitants of that region he has to disguise himself as one of them and in the process succumbs to his environment and forgets his aim. Whereupon his father sends him messengers in the guise of eagles, which, he says, 'alighted beside me and turned into speech'; and he remembers his purpose and after much travail recovers the pearl and returns with it to the court, where he is received with great joy.

These legends have a very practical significance. They indicate that the intelligence of the Divine level has a peculiarly urgent need for the refinement of the coarse materials of the inferior levels; which is why man was created and sent down to the underworld. Underworld it certainly is – a region governed by the laws of temporal cause and effect which humanity at large so grossly misinterprets in terms of self-seeking, and is thereby of negligible individual importance; but the awakening soul has the possibility of *conscious* participation in the events and situations which alters the quality of the experiences.

However, this is only the beginning of the operation for, having learned the technique, the soul is able to produce corresponding transformations of energy in the Astral and Spiritual worlds. The process is not confined to the limited span of earthly life but continues long after death, maybe through several lifetimes. This we will discuss later, but one can envisage that throughout the whole structure there are souls at every level seeking to fulfil their true purpose. Those higher in stature are able to help those who are only beginning the journey; but the important requirement is to start in this life and not wait for a mythical next world.

7

Beyond the Body

The existence of some presence beyond the physical appearance is strikingly confirmed by reports of the sensation of being briefly outside one's body. This is experienced by quite ordinary people, sometimes in a dramatic manner. A friend of mine was once involved in a serious car accident and had a vivid sensation of being present as an onlooker, observing his unconscious body being extricated from the wreckage and taken away in an ambulance.

There are many records of similar experiences, sometimes resulting from some traumatic shock but often in quite ordinary situations.[2, 10] For instance, there is a reported case of a man who was walking along a road with some companions when he became aware of himself hovering above the group with his body still participating in the conversation.[20] Mountaineers and aviators at high altitudes often report vivid out-of-body awareness and the sensation is sometimes experienced under the influence of anaesthetics.

Such experiences are often said to indicate the existence of an 'astral double' which is supposed to reside normally within the body but to become partially dissociated during sleep and even more completely in conditions of trance or shock. It is supposed to be tethered by an invisible cord so that it can rejoin the body when normal conditions are resumed – the 'silver cord' spoken of in Ecclesiastes (xii, 6) which is finally severed at death.

I find a confusion here. The term 'astral double' implies a connection with astral body which is a spiritual entity, whereas out-of-body effects can be, and usually are, entirely physical. As we said earlier, every object in the physical world has a much larger counterpart in the etheric realm. The situation is roughly analogous to that of an iceberg, of which only the tip is visible, the greater part being submerged beneath the surface. Hence everyone can be deemed to possess an etheric body, which is simply that part of the structure which is not detected by the physical senses. The two parts constitute a whole which continues to exist in the phenomenal world as long as it is conducting vital energy. When this is withdrawn at death the physical body disintegrates and the material of the etheric component is dispersed.

Hence the idea that the etheric body can be dissociated from the physical body appears to be a misconception. It is the consciousness which can be detached. Normally this resides virtually entirely in the 'low self' which is centred in the physical body and its varied activities, but it may be raised by a shock of some kind and dwell briefly in the noumenal world from which it can observe the body objectively.

A well developed intuitive mind can induce this state at will if required and mystics regard this as a normal exercise of human faculties; but if this is achieved the potentialities are much greater than the mere sensation of being out of one's body.

The concentration of vital energy in the etheric body can sometimes produce visible manifestations in the form of a fringe or *aura* around the physical body. For a long time these auras were supposed to be visible only to 'sensitives' but recent developments originating from the work of a Russian photographer, Semyon Kirlian, have produced positive and recordable evidence of luminescent patterns surrounding the body, their character depending on the physical and emotional state of the individual.[14]

These auras are not confined to human beings, having been found to be associated with all living matter; but significantly they are not present if the organism is dead, indicating that the vital energy has been dispersed.

Actually the existence of a vital energy pattern within the etheric body was postulated 2,500 years ago by Hippocrates, the 'father' of medicine, who maintained that all illness was due to distortions in this pattern and that physical symptoms were merely the result of attempts by the body's innate intelligence to correct the derangement. The idea was ignored for centuries, but it is beginning to be recognised that the real causes of disease lie in the noumenal world, with which contact can be made through the intuitive faculty.[16]

The etheric body, however, is not a property confined to living matter. Everything has its unmanifest counterpart which exists in the etheric world *throughout its whole history* as a kind of thread in the unseen pattern which can be detected by the paranormal senses. Some people can recognise intuitively the history of an object which they hold in their hands, a technique which is sometimes called psychometry, but a more familiar use of the faculty is the age-old art of divining or dowsing.[14]

This utilises the fact that under suitable conditions the paranormal senses can influence the behaviour of some convenient indicating device such as a hazel twig or a pendulum to which the operator can address (mentally) specific questions. In the hands of an adept clear and unequivocal answers may be obtained. The conventional use of dowsing is in the search for water, but it is equally effective in locating oil and minerals. It has been used to discover archaeological remains or, more spectacularly, missing objects or persons. The practice is fully authenticated and can be regarded as confirming the existence of etheric body.

'You are losing direction,' said my Angel suddenly. 'Paranormal activity is still basically physical and involves only a fractional increase of consciousness. Remember your aim, which was to understand the requirements of *spiritual* progress.'

I saw how the very quality of new ideas can arouse a spurious interest which is self-defeating. The logical mind wants tidy and complete explanations whereas the intuitive mind is content to accept an idea and wait for its details to emerge as the understanding grows.

8

The Soul and the Higher Bodies

I decided to revert to the idea that the earthly body with which one so complacently identifies oneself is really no more than a mechanism for interpreting information from the environment and adapting itself accordingly. It is not to be denigrated on that account, for it is a structure of exquisite precision and intelligence. Yet for what purpose is it provided?

I had been wont to interpret it rather casually as a habitation for a vaguely-imagined soul which was said to emanate from a very high level of the Universe; but I realised that this was a purely abstract idea which needed to be interpreted in much more practical terms. By its very nature it could not be fully understood by the normal intellect, but I remembered that my Angel had told me to stretch my mind in order to prepare a ground in which intuitive understanding could flourish.

Clearly the soul is not to be defined in terms of earthly material. However, it seems that there are differing degrees of materiality and each level of creation has its own quality of existence. In descending scale the successive world orders in the hierarchy are increasingly coarse manifestations of the Supreme

Intelligence which permeates the whole structure; and this means that every level is impregnated with the materials of all the higher levels.

As a rough analogy, we know that physical materials are composed of sub-microscopic atoms, and that these in turn are assemblies of still more infinitesimal electrons, so that the familiar world is permeated by these utterly intangible entities. Yet it is much more significantly impregnated with the incomparably superior materials of the noumenal world, which can only be recognised by the intuitive faculties.

In these terms one can envisage the soul as created out of material of the Divine level to serve as a vehicle for the transmission of consciousness through the structure. For this purpose it permeates all the inferior levels of the hierarchy, in each of which it can display an appropriate quality of consciousness. However, this it has to achieve by individual effort, which is represented in legend as a descent to the level of earth. Here it finds certain crude material which it can refine and utilise for the exploration of successively higher levels in a gradual process of return to its origin. It is a journey in state rather than time, but our minds are so conditioned by the illusion of passing time that we have to think initially in these terms. The significant feature is that at every stage a substantial spiritual payment is required which it has to learn how to make.

When the soul is first conducted down to earth by its guardian angel it has a vestigial memory of the Divine consciousness; but this it is obliged to forget because *it is inappropriate*. It has to accommodate itself to the consciousness of the phenomenal level, for which purpose it inhabits a physical body, and as already said its immediate concern is the establishment of an adequate relationship to the environment. The instinctive functions are already provided by cosmic direction, but the voluntary reactions have to be organised by an individual intelligence. By experience this builds up patterns of associations which thereafter provide automatic interpretations of the impressions received by the senses, so that the body conducts its everyday affairs with no more than a perfunctory direction by the mind.

With this the soul may rest content for a long time, hypnotised by the fascination of life, until it begins to hear the inner promptings – the eagles of the allegory[6] – which remind it of its responsibility. It can then develop deeper levels of the mind which create different ranges of associations and these introduce extra dimensions of understanding. For example, as shown in the previous chapter, it is possible to interpret the information provided by the paranormal senses which recognise the situations in the etheric world, and this constitutes a significant expansion of ordinary consciousness.

However, this is merely the first stage in the development because there are still higher levels of the mind which can communicate with the intelligence of the Astral level, in which there are additional degrees of freedom. We have seen that the ordinary senses can only respond to impressions in sequence, so that everything appears to be changing. Yet actually these successive events are merely interpretations in passing time of an already existing pattern created by the Astral realm, a pattern in which past and future are merely different parts of the region. Situations which appear to the conventional senses as isolated in time and space exist simultaneously at this superior level. As an analogy, the pilot of an aircraft can observe the whole of the territory beneath him and could see, for example, two cars approaching an intersection by different routes in imminent danger of collision, of which the respective drivers would be quite unaware.

Similarly, on a much larger scale, the Astral realm can be envisaged as a region of virtually infinite possibilities, of which a limited number are brought into play by the transit of individual consciousness. Clearly an intelligence operating at this level can be aware in any part of the region and not just the present. This can produce the queer sensations which we sometimes experience, such as an intuitive communion with a friend or relative not physically present, or the feeling of *déja vu* – of having been in some place or situation before – while there are many recorded instances of pre-cognition, usually in dreams. All these experiences can be regarded as quite natural if they are interpreted as brief manifestations of Astral intelligence.

It is significant that these higher states, if they are experienced at all, are usually quite fortuitous and fragmentary. This would seem to be because although the soul has ventured briefly into the Astral realm it has no dwelling place there. It is provided with an organised physical body which it can use for contending with the conditions of earthly life, but it is not supplied with a ready-made astral body. The necessary materials exist, but they have to be assembled in coherent form by individual effort. Moreover, the materials themselves are not available free of charge but, like everything else in the Universe, have to be paid for. Only when these conditions are fulfilled can the soul acquire a second body which it can then use to explore the Astral realm, just as the first (physical) body establishes relationships with the phenomenal world.

What is this necessary payment? It appears to be basically simple, involving the awakening of the dormant levels of the mind which communicate with higher levels of consciousness. These provide interpretations of events beyond the stereotyped reactions of habit, and in so doing create energies of a higher quality which are acceptable currency to the Astral level. This is the real payment, which clearly cannot be made in terms of personal advantage, directed entirely by the low self. There will inevitably be some element of personal aim but this must be accompanied by a clear feeling of dependence on higher authority.

It is not easy to do because of the weight of long-established conventional associations, but to the extent that it is achieved there is a remarkable enrichment of experience. Everything becomes more vivid so that the familiar objects of one's surroundings become alive with new meaning, while one's relationships with other people no longer need the ponderous communication of words.

Perhaps the most significant aspect of this heightened perception is the awareness that everything has its life. This morning, in a moment of quite fortuitous insight, I saw the 'long body' of the tap on my wash basin. Instead of a casual awareness of its present appearance and function I had for a brief instant a glimpse of its whole history from the importation of its raw materials through the fashioning of innumerable craftsmen to its state of usefulness in the house. All these stages are the successive implementation in passing time of a selection of possibilities already existing in the patterns of the Astral realm. This leaves a kind of permanent trace in the eternal fabric which is called the long body, or the time-body, of the object or event.

This may seem to be a trivial and even fanciful example, but in fact every object and event in the physical world has its time-body in the noumenal world, and this includes human beings. Each of us is actualising from moment to moment an already existing pattern in the Astral realm and this leaves a (relatively) permanent trace in the Etheric world. This is what Swedenborg called the Book of Life which is opened at death, the real record of the life containing the causes and relationships of the events which unfold in the world of passing time. However, it is not an inflexible record because the possibilities available are influenced by the levels of consciousness involved. The intelligence of the low self is entirely circumscribed, but the situation can be changed by intelligences of a higher order, as is discussed in Chapter 11.

An important implication of this concept is that nothing exists in isolation. The individual time-body is merely one strand in the interwoven fabric of the noumenal world and is thus influenced by all the other time-bodies in its vicinity. Hence, as John Donne so truly said, 'No man is an island'. Our experiences are inextricably involved with those of our neighbours and even a partly developed astral consciousness will be aware of connections which are not apparent to the limited (and usually self-centred) perceptions of the ordinary mind.

I found it intensely stimulating to realise that the astral body does not come into being fully formed, but has to be developed by conscious effort. It can be regarded as a base for the exploration of the Astral territory, and the better its equipment the wider the possible range of adventure. The soul begins to apprehend with increasing clarity the pattern as a whole and this provides many extra opportunities. It can communicate with other souls in different parts of earthly space and time and may possibly modify its own path through the region.

These opportunities must not be assumed to be available only after death. The material of the astral body has to be collected during life, but once it has been organised, even to a small extent, its perceptions become available immediately. Moreover, as I perceived later, it appears that if the soul has acquired a well formed astral body certain additional opportunities become available, but only if appropriate payment has been made during the life.

The possession of a well organised astral body provides the soul with an interim period of great delight during which it develops its knowledge and understanding of the Astral realm. For a while it may rest content in its new-found freedoms, but in due course it has to use these experiences as material for further progress. This is not automatic, and there are rogue souls which use the facilities for their own ends and thereby reinforce the powers of evil. This dispels the sentimental notion that the soul is inherently 'good'. It is an incomplete creation which is required to perfect itself by voluntary effort; and at every stage there is freedom of choice.

However, if the soul remembers its aim it can begin to organise the formation of a third body which can be used to explore the conditions of the Spiritual world. These are only comprehensible to the deepest levels of the mind which do not use the language of words, but we can envisage that a consciousness at this level can direct the patterns in the Astral realm, and even modify them if necessary. This clearly involves a very high degree of consciousness, for the spiritual body again does not exist ready-made but has to be assembled from the available materials; and we can be sure that this will require a further substantial payment.

The nature of this payment can only be assessed by the intuitive mind. We can assume by inference that it will involve the transformation of the quality of the astral experiences by acknowledging their dependence on a still higher authority, but there appears to be a further factor of peculiar interest. Up to this point the soul's awareness has been individual, but at the Astral level this begins to change. There is a feeling of belonging to all mankind so that the effort to raise the level of consciousness no longer has the same personal significance, but has the quality of compassion. This is a word which is conventionally interpreted in terms of superficial sympathy, but which means literally 'experiencing all together'. Hence the Spiritual level of consciousness not only understands all the lower levels but enters into their manifestations.

One can understand, therefore, that part of the payment for the attainment of this level will be the obligation to help other souls which are in a less advanced state, as is discussed in Chapter 10.

The concept of successively finer bodies seems to be of considerable practical importance. One finds many references to them in occult literature, but it is all too often assumed that they exist as of right. This is incorrect, for, while higher levels of *consciousness* exist, considerable effort is necessary in order to establish a connection with them. This is the soul's task, which is an individual and prolonged endeavour.

It cannot be measured in terms of the days and years of passing time, which are merely an illusion of the senses. Nevertheless, there is an element of duration in the successive levels of the noumenal world each of which is subject to its own time-scale. Hence the exercise must be regarded as extending over a considerable period of astral time; and, as is discussed later, this may occupy many lifetimes of conventional time.

If this sounds intimidating it is because one is still using the limited intelligence of the formatory mind. Seen aright it is a most inspiring adventure in which there is help at every stage once one has learned how to pay. But the most important feature is that it starts, *and can only start*, in life. To wait until after death is useless, for the life simply has to be repeated.

9

Life after Death

The idea that the soul is not fully developed produced a complete change in my attitude to life. I had previously assumed somewhat vaguely that on the death of the body the spirit is immediately reunited with its Maker. I began to suspect that it was not as easy as this and that the sojourn on earth was really part of an exercise of considerable magnitude which might have commenced before I was born and would certainly continue after my death.

The problem was to envisage what this continuing existence might be like and, more specifically, what obligations it might involve while one was still alive. It was, I think, this latter consideration which prompted me to give some serious attention to the matter – which I had previously dismissed as of purely speculative interest.

There is a considerable volume of communications purporting to come from beyond the grave. Some of these are undoubtedly fraudulent, but there are many which have been judged to be genuine by observers of repute. Even so I found them difficult to accept because they appeared always to be couched in the familiar terms of life experience. If the real part of a man or woman resides in a world of a different order, the laws and ordinances of this spiritual realm must be incommensurable with

51

those of the phenomenal world. Hence I felt, as many do, that any description of post-mortem conditions in life terms must, *ipso facto*, be false and to be rejected out of hand.

I put the question to my Angel, who said: 'This is because your judgement is still conditioned by passing time. As long as this is so any communication from the noumenal world must be expressed in these terms if it is to be even partly intelligible. Why do you make this difficulty? You have seen that time does not have the same meaning in the real world, where everything exists eternally, but you do not bring this into your understanding.

'You speak of the soul's journey, knowing this is only an interpretation in everyday language of a change of state. The same applies to life after death, which is not something in the future, but an enlargement of the present.

'But you will not understand this until the noumenal world becomes a reality to you. Meanwhile, study what is said about the hereafter in conventional terms and try to relate it to the ideas which you are beginning to discern with your intuitive mind.'

Conventional thinking assumes that with the death of the body everything associated with it also ceases. Yet the body is merely a mechanism which operates in accordance with directions supplied by a superior intelligence called the mind; and this mind is not part of the physical mechanism so that it survives the death of the body and continues in operation for a while. As the late Dean Matthews said in an address to the Society for Psychical Research (1940, *46*, 15), 'The centre of consciousness in existence during life does not cease to exist after death.'

The influence of this persisting consciousness will depend upon its quality. During life we normally exercise a purely perfunctory attention, confining the operation of the mind to its lowest level, which is concerned only with personal comfort and success. This is utterly inadequate for the development of the soul. After the death of the body it finds itself in the strange

52

new environment of the noumenal world, for which it is usually quite unprepared, and the only intelligence at its disposal is the stereotyped mind which it used so complacently during life.

Swedenborg maintained that the conditions of the afterlife were not greatly different from those on earth, and to a soul which is still trammelled by its earth mind this is how it must appear. It wanders disconsolately through the strange territory trying to orient itself; and it may be a long time before it succeeds in discarding the former associations and is able to respond to the direction of higher levels of intelligence.

Nevertheless, the records of post-mortem experience show a certain consistency. The most impressive are those concerned with what may be called short-term visits by people who have died briefly but have subsequently been revived. Dr Raymond Moody in his book *Life after Life*[10] records a number of such experiences which have interesting similarities.

There appears to be a feeling of lightness and release, with a clear awareness of the body just vacated, though without any coherent understanding of the conditions. Sometimes there is an awareness of other spirits who try to explain what is happening, but it is significant that in many cases the visitor is told that it is necessary to go back because it is not yet time to die.

Longer-term experiences are recounted under conditions of trance. These constitute a less direct but often more comprehensive form of evidence. Again there is frequent reference to guides who help the soul to familiarise itself with the new conditions, and avoid sordid places which could be regarded as incorrect interpretations by the still-active earth mind.

Maurice Nicoll used to point out a very particular aspect of this situation, namely that the period of readjustment can be considerably reduced by conscious effort while one is still alive. The low mind is created to co-ordinate the information provided by the senses and so contend with the events of life; but it becomes contaminated with a host of personal associations – of pride and vanity, conceit and intolerance – which are of no value to the soul's real purpose and only give rise to discontent and unhappiness. These spurious associations can be sacrificed without any detriment whatsoever, leaving the mind free from unnecessary clutter; but this is much more difficult to do after death because the impressions of the physical world are no longer available and a painful re-education has to be undertaken. Swedenborg reports conversations with angels who ask the soul if it is ready to die; but one would suspect that only a conscious soul could answer this.

There is a problem here, for in all these operations there appears to be an element of time. Yet there are evidently different orders of time and we shall not expect to measure the soul's progress in terms of the passing time of the senses. It is said that each level in the hierarchy has its own time-scale which is virtually infinite in terms of the level below.[12] Hence for us the Astral realm is timeless and eternal.

As was said earlier, the events of life can be regarded as brought into being by a transit of consciousness in passing time through an already existing pattern in the Astral world, in which pattern the span of earthly existence occupies a very small part. The soul's adventure is an excursion through the whole of this realm and consequently extends both before and after the life of the physical body, though in its own time it will be of finite duration.

The conditions have to be envisaged with the intuitive mind, which can comprehend the Astral and physical levels together. It will be able to interpret situations in terms of the passing time of the senses where this is appropriate, and yet can understand that at the higher level the present and the future – and the past – are co-existing aspects of the real pattern.

It is evident that the discontinuity which we call death should not be regarded with despair, but should be met with unusual awareness. This is the purpose of the last rites traditionally administered to a dying person in some religions, while in ancient times specific procedures were prescribed for dying, as one finds in the Egyptian or Tibetan Books of the Dead.[3] According to these, the period immediately following the death of the body is one of great confusion because the soul no longer has any habitation and exists for a time in a limbo of uncertainty. It does not realise that its former body has ceased to function and attempts to derive meaning from memories of life experiences.

This period of readjustment is called the *bardo* and is said to last for forty days. This is a symbolic figure since in esoteric language the figure forty is used to denote a period of spiritual regeneration, as for example in the forty days and nights spent by Moses on Mount Sinai before coming down with the tables of the sacred law, or the withdrawal into the wilderness for forty days by Christ prior to his temptation by the Devil.

In earthly time it may endure for years. Maurice Nicoll once said of a colleague who had died three years previously, 'B. has just realised he is dead.' There are instances where the purification has not been possible for generations. On the other hand, if there has been a successful creation of an astral body during earthly life, the period in the bardo may be very short.

Neither in life nor after death is the soul expected or even able to raise its own level. Individual effort is certainly required but this has to involve the acknowledgement and acceptance of help from higher levels of consciousness; and this is always available when properly called on.

In this context it is significant that many post-mortem communications speak of being met by other souls who act as guides through the bardo region. These are necessarily personalised, often in the form of people previously encountered in life. They help the newcomer to recognise the squalid places in the territory and move into more pleasant locations where it may meet other souls from whom further help is possible. By all accounts, merely to wish to move in this psychological territory is sufficient. There is no lapse of time, which is confusing to the soul still shackled by earthly associations, but it is characteristic of Astral travel in general, as one would expect in these timeless realms.

I find this idea of being met inspiring, since it confirms what has been stated earlier, namely that we do not exist in isolation. One can surmise that certain souls are delegated to meet new-comers as a form of further payment, which I shall discuss in the next chapter. But the idea has more immediate implications for there are fellow souls on earth with whom we can communicate, and maybe give or receive help.

These spiritual neighbours, however, cannot be recognised by the low mind, which is concerned basically with desires. The ordinary ties of affection between friends and lovers, parents and children, are significant only at earth level and have no permanent validity unless there is also a spiritual affinity; and conversely one may find a kindred spirit in a person to whom one is not physic-ally attracted. If the attention can be withdrawn from the egregious demands of the low self, the higher levels of the mind may establish communication with the astral bodies of our real neighbours.

A particular aspect of this situation is the possibility of com-munication with people who have just died. All too often one's reactions are of personal bereavement and distress. With a little more awareness we could understand the situation of the departed soul and remain in contact with it during its inevitable early confusion. To do this we have to remember them with all the love and affection at our command – but no regret, which only adds to their burden.

Gurdjieff, speaking of the unexpected death of his colleague Orage, bitterly condemned the mass of insincere condolences which had poured in. Such utterances, he said, did great harm to the departed soul, rekindling its suffering, and in ancient times were considered immoral and criminal.

10

Communication with the Noumenal World

For many years I accepted the concept of the unmanifest world, which I felt intuitively to be right. Not only did it appear to contain the underlying patterns of the events of life, but it presupposed an intelligence and purpose far beyond human imagining. But it was an academic awareness and I began to feel the need to recognise the presence of the noumenal world as a reality in which I was an actual participant. I was led, apparently by accident, to an appreciation of the extent to which it is possible to communicate with, and be guided by, the superior intelligences of this realm.

Many of us experience such contact without realising it, usually in dreams. Dreaming is an activity which takes place when the normal attention is relaxed, as in sleep. In these conditions the brain still receives information from various sources, external and internal, and this it endeavours to interpret by the use of the familiar associations of habit, resulting in a garbled succession of imaginary experiences. Such dreams are of little significance, save as indications of suppressed, and possibly unconscious anxiety which should ideally be cancelled before going to sleep.

A more important aspect of the dream state, however, is that it permits the reception of information from other than the physical world. Influences from the noumenal world are continually impinging upon us but are normally ignored because the low mind, which preponderates during the waking state, cannot understand them. When this level of the mind becomes quiescent (either naturally or by volition) it becomes possible for higher levels to operate and provide interpretations of these finer impressions which result in dreams of a different and more significant quality.

The brain is still only able to translate the information in conventional form, so that in the dreams one meets and converses with physical images of people. But this is no longer insignificant, as it is with ordinary dreams, which are merely an expression of suppressed desires. We have seen that the noumenal world contains the time-bodies of all the people (and events) in the psychological country so that communication is possible with and from those in the immediate vicinity.

This is amply confirmed in practice. Almost everyone has experience of unsolicited dream conversations with someone with whom they are spiritually in rapport. Moreover, these experiences are often clairvoyant, containing an element of precognition, so that one is aware of some impending trouble – or maybe good fortune – for a relative or friend. All this is entirely consistent with the concept of interwoven time-bodies in the fabric of the noumenal world.

These experiences are usually haphazard, occurring at random for no obvious reason; but this need not be so. They arise from the operation of naturally existing traces of higher levels of the mind which are normally starved because all the available energy is squandered in a quite disproportionate attention to the activities of the low mind. If some of this unnecessary attention can be withdrawn, the higher levels are automatically nourished and begin to develop their proper potentiality.

There are some people in whom these faculties are naturally

well established, possibly as a result of payments made in previous lives. They are said to be 'fey', or to possess second sight, which we are apt to regard as some kind of abnormality. Actually it is a faculty which develops quite naturally as the mind begins to awaken, but this cannot be achieved by mere wishing. The attention has to be increasingly withdrawn from the *unnecessary* demands of the low self – the spurious feeling I mentioned in Chapter 4. To the extent that this is achieved the intuitive mind begins to create a heightened awareness which is not confined to dreams but can operate during the waking state. One sees beneath the surface and begins to recognise the real relationships which exist in the noumenal world between the isolated people and events of one's ordinary awareness.

This is a state of clairvoyance resulting from the expanded consciousness which is released when the clamour of the low mind is stilled. It is really a natural faculty which has fallen into disuse due to the preoccupation with materialism. It produces a state of detachment which is not only psychological but can permit the consciousness to be withdrawn for a time from the physical body as in the out-of-body states discussed in Chapter 7. If a well organised astral body has been formed, communication is possible not only with souls still inhabiting the earth but also with others within the Astral realm.

Still greater possibilities exist if a spiritual body has been organised, since through this medium contact may be made with advanced souls who may impart something of the real knowledge preserved in what are called the Akashic records. Akasha is a Sanskrit word describing the fundamental unmanifest fabric of the Universe in which lie the real causes of the successive manifestations, and it is these sources which inspire the esoteric teaching promulgated by the saints and mystics through the ages.

At such a level the discarnate spirit can visit the regions of the Spiritual world. This is relatively rare during earthly experience but there is evidence in the annals of the Theosophical Society confirming the possibility. The Indian mystic Kishnamurti mentions meetings in an out-of-body state with members of the Conscious Circle of Humanity, from whom he received certain initiation; but this involved very substantial payment, including considerable physical distress.[9]

In addition to these individual experiences there are other forms of communication which are objective in character, in that the recipient of the information is not personally involved, except as a medium through whom the influences can operate. It is of much less common occurrence because relatively few people have the ability to provide the necessary link with the noumenal world.

In the majority of cases the medium goes into a trance, which is a state of voluntary coma. The attention is completely withdrawn from the physical body, which continues to function naturally under the direction of its instinctive intelligence but becomes to all outward appearance unconscious. The low mind is thus rendered quiescent, which permits the intuitive mind to interpret information being imparted by higher levels of consciousness.

The form of communication varies widely both in character and quality. Sometimes the medium speaks with the voice of its supposed 'control'. Alternatively, some mechanical device such as a planchette may be used to answer questions or even to spell out messages letter by letter. The use of a mechanical aid does not necessarily invalidate the manifestation. It is akin to the action of the forked rod or pendulum which the dowser uses to interpret paranormal influences, but it is essential to ensure that the interpretations are not adulterated by any form of voluntary direction.

This is not easy, particularly when groups of people gather together in a seance. Apart from the possibility of trickery, which is easily contrived even under apparently rigorous supervision, the exercise all too often starts from a wrong premise, namely the desire to obtain answers to personal problems. The mind of the medium is in a very vulnerable condition because with its formatory part quiescent it is open to influences not only from the noumenal world but also the subconscious aspirations of the questioner. These may be very strong and can easily overpower the more delicate spiritual influences so that any answers which emerge will be of a very mundane quality.

Experience shows that the powers of a medium develop with practice. It is as if some kind of apprenticeship has to be served, during the early stages of which only a very pedestrian response is available, such as spelling out answers letter by letter; and any irreverent experiments will never get beyond this stage, nor will their answers have any authenticity. With practice, however, a genuine medium will learn to ignore spurious influences and achieve a purity of mind which can provide significant interpretations of higher intelligence. This is the true exercise of the faculty which permits understanding to be conveyed from a higher to a lower level for the fulfilment of cosmic purposes.

An example of this kind of experience is to be found in Jane Sherwood's record of communications from T. E. Lawrence (Lawrence of Arabia).[18] Mrs Sherwood is a medium of the highest quality, but it is interesting to note that this facility did not appear overnight. She had always been convinced of the continuity of existence, but her ideas gave her little comfort on the death of her husband. She was urged to attend spiritualist seances, which she did with some distaste, finding them overlaid with sentimental jargon. Yet she was impelled by inner promptings (which she felt intuitively were instigated by her husband) to continue the search and ultimately met a woman who suggested that she should experiment with a planchette.

This is a small trolley with a pencil at one end on which one rests the hand lightly and waits for it to move. It is again akin to the dowser's pendulum and if the mind is quiescent it can move in a meaningful manner. This proved to be the case for Mrs Sherwood, as she describes in her book *The Country Beyond*,[17] and in due course she developed an extraordinary facility with this instrument which wrote long and intelligible sentences 'spoken' by the soul with whom she was in contact.

The writings confirm the interim experience of the soul in the bardo mentioned in the previous chapter. Lawrence reports his confusion in becoming aware of his dead body beside the motor cycle on which he met his fatal accident and his subsequent meetings with other souls who guided him through the new territory.[18] However, the accounts go far beyond this and describe, as far as is possible in words, the much more coherent experiences in the Astral realm which can be inhabited when the purification of the mind has been accomplished.

This is characteristic of genuine post-mortem communications (of which many other records exist). They are concerned with the transmission of ideas which can dispel the obscurities of earthly existence and indicate how the proper use may be made of the opportunities provided. It appears, moreover, that this is an essential part of the cosmic plan, an obligation which has to be undertaken by more advanced souls in the course of their own development.

A remarkable example of this obligation is recounted in Helen Greaves's book *The Wheel of Eternity*.[4] Mrs Greaves is not a professional medium but possesses an unusual psychic sensitivity. She describes how she came to live in an old and charming cottage and was surprised one evening to become aware of an old woman sitting opposite. Though initially somewhat apprehensive she gradually made contact with this phantom and discovered after several visitations that it was the spirit of a woman who used to live in that same cottage and had been the maid to the mistress of a big house nearby.

It was not a happy life, for the mistress was a selfish and petulant married woman who had been seduced by her gardener and gave birth to a half-wit son whom she utterly rejected and who was later drowned in a local pond. (It transpired subsequently that there was some historical confirmation of these events.)

One evening some time later she became aware of a presence in the room so she switched off her TV set and waited, when two people appeared. One announced himself as the spirit of the boy, no longer enchained in a defective body, and introduced the other as a Brother of Light in charge of the group of souls to which the boy belonged. This was the beginning of an extraordinary succession of visitations, which ultimately included the mistress, as a result of which both she and the maid were cleansed of the lingering shackles of their life personality and released to continue their real journey.

This is no more than a brief précis of a very moving narrative which is of peculiar interest as indicating how souls may remain earthbound for centuries by the persisting influence of evil habits. Moreover, it seems that this does not affect only the principal offender. The maid in the story appears to have been of a good and kindly disposition, but was entirely engulfed in the miasma of self-will and hatred of the mistress. The boy, protected by the limited intelligence of his defective body, not only escapes this contamination but is able in due course to return with appropriate help.

Here is compassion indeed, an awareness that the mother, whose soul had not yet awakened, had been behaving in the only way possible for her. If we, in our self-centred arrogance, could display a similar understanding we might begin to release not only ourselves but our neighbours, while still in life.

Contact with the noumenal world is not limited to the transmission of ideas. It can sometimes be applied in a very practical manner to the treatment of physical ailments. As said earlier, illness is a symptom of disharmony in the pattern of vital energy in the etheric world; but it is this pattern which directs the continuous replenishment of the cells of the body. Hence if it can be altered to correct any derangements the bodily tissues will revert to normal.

Such a modification can be effected by a consciousness operating at the Astral level and there are people who can conduct this force and produce apparently miraculous cures. Few people possess this gift and they are the first to admit that it is not they who produce the results but a force acting through them. Similar cures may sometimes be obtained by visiting places in which there is a high concentration of *mana*, such as the pool at Lourdes.

Alternatively, healing may be provided through a medium who can establish contact with the Astral intelligence. A remarkable exponent of this technique in recent times was the American psychic Edgar Cayce. Born in 1877 in Hopkinsville, Kentucky, of simple farming stock, he led an undistinguished life until he was twenty-one, when he was afflicted with laryngitis and lost his voice. His doctors were unable to cure him and he became despondent. By chance he met a hypnotist who put him into a trance, during which he not only diagnosed the cause of his affliction but suggested a quite unorthodox treatment which proved completely effective. Yet on awakening from the trance he had neither memory nor knowledge of the diagnosis.

From this there developed a remarkable history which is recorded in detail by Gina Cerminara in her book *Many Mansions*.[1] He was persuaded to try to develop this talent for the benefit of other people, to which he agreed reluctantly on the condition that he should receive no money for anything he did. Having been introduced to a patient he would go into a trance during which he prescribed appropriate treatment, sometimes involving previously unknown medicaments and often at variance with orthodox prescriptions.

As time progressed he developed a clairvoyant faculty which enabled him to treat patients at a distance, provided he was given some object or information which could establish a rapport. From casual remarks which he made in these sessions in was evident that his spirit was actually present at the distant scene. He would describe the condition of the patient and make his prognosis, which was duly recorded by his attendant because he himself had no recollection of his utterances when he awoke.

Later he began to become aware of the time-bodies of ancient civilisations such as Atlantis, which still exist in the etheric world, and his utterances became increasingly concerned with such legends. He died in 1945, having become something of a legend himself.

An interesting variant of the art is described by Bernard Hutton in his book *Healing Hands.*[7] He records his experiences with a medium, George Chapman, who in his trance condition speaks with the voice of Dr Lang, an eminent surgeon who died in 1937. Following a successful treatment for incipient blindness Dr Lang explained how he, with a group of similarly qualified spirits, had sought for and educated a suitable medium – George Chapman – through whom they could contact patients and manipulate their etheric bodies.

I find this an interesting idea which suggests that Astral communication is not as accidental as it might appear but may be directed by discarnate souls in the fulfilment of their own development. One can envisage that the Universe may be populated by a large number of souls in different states of being, some in the process of descent from the Divine level of their creation, others at various stages of return – an idea portrayed in the well-known vision of the patriarch Jacob in which he saw a ladder set between heaven and earth on which were angels ascending and descending.

One can surmise further that at every stage of the ascent an appropriate payment is required. Initially this is the effort to awaken the deeper levels of the mind but once this has been achieved a further and continuing payment is necessary. This appears to be of an increasingly impersonal quality which involves an obligation to help other souls on their respective journeys. Some may be required to maintain the constant supply of esoteric ideas on earth, represented in the medieval *Mutus Liber* as angels blowing trumpets in the ear of a sleeping figure. Others may be assigned to meet souls newly arrived in the bardo after the death of their physical body, or maybe to make contact in dreams with souls still in life.

At a more advanced stage a soul may perhaps be commissioned to provide specific communication through a suitable medium; and this, of course, would involve the discovery and subsequent education of an individual possessing the necessary sensitivity. There seems to me here to be a design of great majesty, confirming the conviction that we do not exist in isolation.

There are many matters of detail on which one can speculate. Why are some people given the facility to act as mediums? Even more pertinently, what arbitrary dispensation permits some people to receive spiritual healing while others equally deserving do not?

'Why do you always want explanations?' said my Angel. 'These events are all part of the pattern created by the Astral intelligence in which the roles allotted to different individuals always contain the most appropriate opportunities for their real development. Can you not let your intuitive mind savour the wonder of the design which has contrived that communication shall be continually available between the spiritual and material levels?'

11

Repeated Lives

Most of us have an innate belief that life is not an end in itself and that in some way the experience will continue after death under different and possibly more favourable conditions. It is a comfortable but very superficial philosophy because life has a purpose beyond the complacent acceptance of the succession of events.

According to legend the soul descends to the level of earth in order to produce a certain refinement of the energies which exist there by *conscious* participation in the widely varied events. To the extent that this is achieved it begins to grow in stature, but the more important aspect of the endeavour is that these refined energies provide a special kind of nourishment for the higher levels of the hierarchy, which is, indeed, the reason for the creation of man in the Universe.

This is evidently a task of considerable magnitude. The soul has to learn to subordinate its individual ambitions to the cosmic requirements, and it seems unlikely that this can be fully achieved within the brief span of earthly life. It is probably the intuitive awareness of this limitation that prompts the vague belief in a future existence. Yet to accept this without question is to evade the issue entirely.

Is one to assume an indefinite succession of further lives in store; and what has been the purpose and value of the present life? Conventional thinking regards events as passing for ever into the limbo of the past, never to return. But each and every event involves the expenditure of energy and to suppose that this energy is continually running to waste is quite incompatible with the concept of an intelligent and economical Universe.

In some way events must be re-used, but this cannot be understood in terms of the conventional sense of time. There is, however, a simple solution if one postulates that the transits of consciousness through the noumenal pattern are circular so that in due time everything is repeated. This is the idea of eternal recurrence which is of great antiquity and is certainly derived from akashic knowledge. It has been discussed by many writers, notably by Maurice Nicoll in his classic book *Living Time*.[13] At all points of time, he says, things are being refashioned.

One can see how the events of life do not just lapse into oblivion with the passage of time but remain in existence in the etheric pattern, from which they can be reactivated by a fresh transit of consciousness. This is the *palingenesis* (again becoming) of the Stoic philosophy, according to which everything comes into being, serves its purpose, dies and is reborn – an idea which is in accord with the concept of continuous creation which was discussed earlier.

Even so, the concept of recurrence remained for me merely an intriguing theory until I suddenly perceived that it is an absolutely necessary element in the scheme. It is part of the mechanism of replenishment, discussed earlier, whereby the energies passing down the hierarchy of world orders from the Creator are returned in modified form at each stage by the processes of transformation. It is a living process so that the phenomenal world created by the Astral intelligence is continually being reactivated by recurring transits of a wide variety of consciousnesses operating in many different but interrelated ways. At each transit there is produced a fresh supply of transformed energy so that the Universe is constantly being replenished.

This continual reactivation of the existing material is taking place on many scales simultaneously, some occupying aeons of our time. This is depicted in the vision of Ezekiel (Chapter x) who saw the spiritual universe as a structure of wheels within wheels. Within this vast pattern is man, who is a special creation equipped with the possibility of exercising an individual consciousness. His body is created and maintained by cosmic intelligence, but the soul which inhabits it has an independent existence which possesses different degrees of freedom. It can, in particular, undergo an *individual* recurrence within the cosmic pattern by re-inhabiting the body at the point of its physical birth and repeating the life more intelligently.

The idea is usually grossly misinterpreted in terms of a mythical 'next time' in which one can, with the experience gained the previous time, conduct oneself with greater merit and perhaps avoid the less pleasant incidents altogether. This is the acme of complacency, being neither correct nor intelligent. The experience which one fondly imagines will be helpful 'next time' is part of the artificially acquired personality which has to be completely discarded before the soul can continue its progress. However, if during life the soul has developed some awareness of the underlying pattern in the noumenal world this trace of real memory may allow the events to be interpreted more consciously, in which case the repetition would have some meaning.

Hence it seems to me that the possibility of a *significant* recurrence is not an automatic right but is available only if an acceptable payment has been made by conscious effort during life.

The idea of payment is implicit in Plato's Myth of Er, mentioned earlier. After the death of the body the soul has first to be purified by removing the contamination of the life personality, after which it is brought before the Judges who assess its performance during the sojourn on earth. If there has been no conscious effort the soul may be condemned to re-live the same life, born of the same parents in the same circumstances. This is what is called absolute recurrence, maintaining the pattern of earthly manifestation simply to fulfil the requirements of the phenomenal world. At each recurrence the soul will receive decreasing nourishment from the environment so that it ultimately dies.

This thought is shattering to one's complacency. Yet the soul is not forever immortal. It is created immature, a spiritual child which needs to be nourished in exactly the same manner as a physical child. The food is always available but the soul has to extract and digest it by its own efforts. Of this it is constantly reminded by esoteric influences – the angels with the trumpets mentioned in the previous chapter – but if it fails to respond, or chooses poisonous food, it may become utterly emaciated, and will die unless it is redeemed by advanced souls.

However, if the soul has made some effort to awaken during the life it may develop a certain amount of real memory, which might produce a greater awareness of some of the situations. The physical circumstances will not be appreciably altered because the various roles still have to be played as before but the quality of the experience can be changed.

It must be remembered that events include all the psychological reactions of the people involved in the occurrence and so are much more flexible than the physical happenings. A slightly different path through the noumenal pattern may completely change an event without disturbing its external manifestation. For example, I shall still meet the man who arouses in me such intense antagonism but with a greater understanding our clashes can take place without the former rancour. I can, indeed, cancel the bitterness now, which will actually change the supposedly irretrievable past.

Once the soul has begun to awaken, its memory becomes progressively stronger with succeeding recurrences until the whole role is played consciously. Maurice Nicoll calls this the consummation of the life, which may permit the allotment of a fresh role.[13] The most inspiring aspect of the situation, however, is that any conscious effort affects not only myself but all the other people involved in the event (who may or may not take advantage of the opportunity). It is clear, in fact, that man does not live to himself alone. What I do affects my neighbour, not necessarily in the external world but more significantly in the noumenal pattern through which we are all passing in our individual transits.

The *conscious* repetition of the life may result in the acquisition of sufficient spiritual money to buy an entirely different life. This would not be with the object of escaping from difficulties but in search of further opportunities for development. For this to be permitted the Assessors must be satisfied that a competent use has been made of the existing life and that there has been formed a reasonably mature astral body (which in itself may require several recurrences).

If the requirements are met, the soul may be permitted to choose a fresh life (within its price range), but this is only possible if there is another soul ready to occupy the former body and also if the soul at present inhabiting the new life is sufficiently qualified to leave it (or maybe has made such poor use of its opportunities as to warrant demotion). One can surmise that there may be a period of waiting before the requisite conditions can be met.

One can envisage a constant transference of souls throughout the system to permit the full use of the available psychological material. Any given life can only provide a limited range of opportunities and the soul has to learn to contend with all types of experience. According to astrological lore it is necessary to pass through all the signs of the Zodiac in order to complete the circle of earthly experience, while Gurdjieff maintained that roles had to be interchanged so that the master becomes the slave, the executioner the victim, and so forth. The allotment, of course, is in the hands of the Assessors, though there may be some element of choice if sufficient payment has been made.

There is, however, an aspect of the situation which has immediate implications. It was said that a fresh life can only be occupied when its existing tenant is able to vacate it. It may well be that there is a soul waiting to inhabit one's own life, but unable to do so because one has not yet made sufficient payment to allow it to be vacated. It is said that no one can play a fresh role until he has made possible his own replacement; which reminds us that our obligation is not just to ourselves.

The occupancy of a different life amounts to what is called reincarnation. The word has acquired a speciously dramatic connotation associated with reputed memories of previous existences but this is too limited an interpretation. Any tenancy of a new body is a reincarnation, and is not an uncommon occurrence though it is largely unrecognised because in the ordinary course there is no recollection of the previous life. This is because the ordinary memory is a function of the Personality which has to be eradicated before any spiritual progress can be made.

However, a consciousness at the Astral level will be aware of the pattern of history as a whole and may recognise the time-bodies of any previous lives. In many cases the soul will be fully occupied with the present life unless the previous reincarnation is of particular significance. It is worthy of note that many of these recollections are of periods of hardship or of cruelty which could produce massive scars on the time-body and hence obtrude into the consciousness.

A 'previous' life is not necessarily in the past of historical time. It may be in the contemporary era or even in some future period. Memory in this case, however, would be more difficult because it would involve situations and conditions which have not yet developed in time.

There are, nevertheless, people who appear to have clear recollections of previous incarnations which are sometimes found to have remarkable authenticity. Such a case is recorded by Dr Arthur Guirdham in his book *The Cathars and Reincarnation.*[5] It is an account of discussions over a period of years with a patient, to whom he was introduced by chance, who has vivid memories of her life in thirteenth-century France. She belonged to a heretical sect known as the Cathars who were repressed by the Inquisition in a reign of terror which wasted Languedoc for a century. Her memories were not only very detailed but incorporated many corrections to the historical records, which were subsequently verified.

There are many examples of this kind of recollection, not all of them so readily authenticated, but none the less genuine. Their clarity and vividness suggests an interesting possibility, namely that the relevant historical period is actually being inhabited together with the life in the present era. One can envisage that a soul with a fully developed Astral consciousness would have no difficulty in inhabiting several lives at once, a possibility which is mentioned by Ouspensky and others, which would clearly increase the opportunities of extracting the maximum nourishment from earthly experience; but one can surmise that this will only be permitted in exchange for very considerable spiritual payment.

Still greater possibilities appear to exist for souls which have attained a consciousness at the spiritual level. These will be what Schuré called the Great Initiates who visit earth as saints and mystics. Ouspensky suggests that some may be commissioned to reincarnate as historical figures and might, with the hindsight of subsequent experience, alter the course of events. The possibilities are evidently small but he says that no real evolution for humanity can be contemplated unless the opportunity exists for individual souls to go into the past and struggle against the causes of present evil.[11]

The influence of previous recurrences is expressed in the idea of karma, which is often erroneously identified with retribution. The Law of Karma states quite simply that the experiences of the present life are generated by a transit in time through a pattern already established in a previous recurrence. The pattern is not entirely individual but is affected by other people involved who may introduce influences of violence and evil. In the absence of any conscious direction these influences acquire a certain endurance so that the life is entirely dominated by this previous conditioning which constitutes the karma.

It is clear that the karma is not immutable. Even a small degree of consciousness will enable the soul to traverse a different path through the astral fabric which will begin to release it from the burden of the past, and this is its task in life.

In these terms there is nothing grim or distasteful in the ideas of karma and recurrence. On the contrary, they are a source of inspiration if we can assess them with the intuitive mind and not encumber the understanding with problems of detail. The most practical aspect of the ideas is their reaffirmation of the necessity for payment, by appropriate effort, if the possibilities are to be properly realised; and it is a payment which one has to start to make while still on earth – not in some conveniently remote hereafter.

12

Conscious Immortality

Indian philosophy says that we live in a world of illusion. In one sense this is literally true because the word is derived from *ludere*, meaning to play a game; and we know that the whole of the phenomenal world is a structure operating in accordance with clearly defined rules. But the word has the secondary meaning of a deception, a belief based on a limited perception of the truth, and it is clear that conventional interpretations based solely on the evidence of the senses fall within this category.

The greatest of our illusions appears to be the assumption that there is always sufficient time. We know intuitively that any real goal must be forever just beyond our reach. The meaning lies in the pursuit rather than in the attainment. Yet we take it for granted that there will always be the opportunity, if not now at least in some imagined future state.

'You have doubts?' said my Angel.

'Yes,' I answered, 'because the element of payment seems to be missing. One assumes vaguely that the spirit is immortal. Yet is this not something which above all has to be earned?'

'True,' he agreed, 'but there are different qualities of immortality. There is a mechanical immortality and there is a conscious immortality. Try to think about this for yourself.'

As so often before, he had provided the clue. We speak glibly of the immortal soul. Yet what do we mean by immortality? Superficially it is interpreted as survival beyond the span of mortal life; but it is also traditionally associated with the eternal life of the gods which would seem to be of a different quality from mere survival. It is evident, in fact, that within the hierarchy of levels in the Universe there are differing degrees of eternity. Each world order has its own quality of consciousness and manifestation, and in particular its own time-scale. This means that objects and events which have a finite life at one level exist continuously in the pattern of the level above. The Astral level is, for us, eternal, but it is still subject to the laws of its own time. Hence eternity (and immortality) are not absolute but depend on the order of consciousness involved.

Since all physical appearances are manifestations of an already existing pattern in the noumenal realm, all living creatures will have an immaterial counterpart in the etheric world which in terms of the passing time of the senses will be immortal; but this etheric counterpart is not spiritual in character, being merely the unmanifest part of the phenomenal world created by the Astral intelligence. Hence organic life in general has a purely functional and limited immortality arising simply from the much longer time-scale of the Astral level. The patterns continue to exist even though the physical presentation has passed, and the same applies to inanimate objects in their sphere.

The human soul is of a different order, being a living entity in its own right. It is created out of Divine material, but in an embryo state and has to complete itself by acquiring experience in each of the inferior levels in the hierarchy. This is its food for, like a physical child, it requires nourishment if it is to grow.

However, it has to learn to assimilate this food and this does not happen automatically. The physical body absorbs and digests its food instinctively, but a specific effort is required to digest psychological food. The events and experiences exist but they provide no spiritual nourishment until they are consciously acknowledged. This is the payment which the soul has to make if it is to grow – and in so doing fulfil its obligation to its Creator. There is a small growth during early childhood when the sense of wonder and delight is predominant, but in the ordinary course this quickly gives place to preoccupation with worldly affairs, and if the soul surrenders to this hypnotism it loses its individuality and merges with the impersonal pattern of the Astral world which is concerned only with cosmic requirements. In such conditions the soul is condemned to an eternal repetition of the same experiences through repeated lives until it either learns to awaken or gradually dies. This constitutes what Ouspensky calls 'byt', a mass of people who play roles of unchangeable routine as part of the already established order.[11] It may include persons of distinction who sway the destinies of nations but are compelled to play their roles without variation in order to maintain the continuity of history. Evidently there is here a purely cosmic and impersonal immortality.

The situation is different if the soul remembers its aim. It realises that it is only *visiting* the Astral realm in the course of its journey, and can begin to use the events of life as material for the organisation of a second (astral) body which will serve as a vehicle for a more objective and individual consciousness. This forms a kind of dwelling place within the Astral realm from which the soul can explore the territory as a whole and understand the reasons for the disconnected events of life. This will involve an immortality of a superior order since by the conscious participation in the experiences the soul transcends the mechanical requirements of the Astral level and is able to use the facilities individually.

Similarly, with persistence, third and fourth bodies may be organised through which to explore the Spiritual and Divine levels and these will clearly possess successively prolonged immortality. This can be regarded as a succession of stages on the return journey, and Christ speaks of the 'many mansions' in his Father's house (John xiv, 2). The word in the Greek (monē) has the meaning of a stopping-place or stage.

It was said earlier, however, that the journey of the soul is a progress in state, rather than time, and the successive stages should really be interpreted in these terms. This becomes more readily understood within the concept of different degrees of immortality. The spiritual worlds accessible to man form a kind of ladder in which each level in the ascent contains an additional dimension.

This means, for example, that all the objects and events in the material world exist all together in the Astral realm. Hence a consciousness at Astral level will be aware *simultaneously* of all the separate manifestations in the phenomenal world. This is indicated in the comment of Christ in a discourse on anxiety – 'Are not two sparrows sold for a farthing; and not one of them shall fall on the ground without your Father' (Matthew x, 29). The wording in the original has the implication of awareness, indicating that the events of life are all known to and understood by a higher level of consciousness. Spiritual and Divine levels will have an even more comprehensive awareness, utterly incommensurable with human understanding.

In the present context, however, the significant aspect of these higher levels of consciousness is that they are outside the passing time of the senses. This means that the organisation of the higher bodies is not an exercise which can be attempted only after the death of the physical body, but is a continuing task during the existing life.

I began to perceive a situation which my intuitive mind had been endeavouring to clarify for some time. One regards one's life as a brief excursion within the physical world, which we accept as an inevitable condition of existence. However, the real participant in the adventure is the soul, which is using the body to extract information from the earthly surroundings.

As it learns to use this material consciously it is able to create higher (extra-physical) bodies through which it can explore the Astral and Spiritual realms while still inhabiting the physical body; and this is an adventure which it can repeat many times until it has utilised the opportunities to the full. As was said in the previous chapter, it is not the body which recurs, but the consciousness which inhabits it. During its lifespan the body can be directed by all the available levels of consciousness *simultaneously*.

The conventional idea of a 'hereafter' is, in fact, an illusion of logical thinking which is inexorably conditioned by the sense of passing time. The intuitive mind, free from this limitation, can recognise the mystical return to the Source as an exercise which involves the integration of experience extending throughout all the eternally existing patterns of the Universe, and that this is something which can take place *now*.

I saw too that the exercise is concerned with growth of understanding, which is quite different from mere knowledge. Much of the literature on the supposed hereafter contains detailed accounts of post-mortem conditions which I feel can be accepted only with reservations. They are necessarily expressed in words and can by that very fact be only partial representations of the truth; but the more important reason is that details of this kind are of no value as such. They only stimulate idle speculation and reinforce the illusion of a future state wherein all will be revealed.

Any real understanding can only be purchased in the present. For too long we rest content in the vague 'assurance of things hoped for' which we call faith. We have to go beyond this comfortable hope and make room for the conscious enjoyment of present opportunities. If this can be done we are no longer hypnotised by the future but know that now is the time – and the only time.

13

The State of Enlightenment

I found an increasing delight in the awareness of the moment. The events of the day and the impressions of the environment acquire a kind of impersonal quality, not concerned with the future (or the past), in which everything becomes alive with meaning. Gurdjieff expressed this as a feeling of 'I here now', which frees the soul from the hypnotism of passing time.

This is the Nirvana of Buddhist philosophy, which is not a mystical future goal but is defined as a state of enlightenment in which the mind is free from its habitual conditioning and is no longer concerned with progress in time.[8] The idea was expressed even more explicitly by Christ in the well-known saying 'The Kingdom of God is at hand'. This is usually interpreted as implying the approaching fulfilment of the prophecies but the phrase 'at hand' really has the meaning of within or all around.

This state of enlightenment is not a remote possibility. It is attainable here and now, but because of the weight of habitual associations it is at first experienced only in brief moments of bliss, and even then only by listening to the inner levels of the mind which are constantly inspired by more conscious levels of the Universe. In Christian terminology this is called repentance, a word which is conventionally interpreted as implying regret for past misdeeds (from the Latin *paenitere*), which is a futile exercise; but there is a more correct derivation from *pensito*, which means to weigh very carefully, or to ponder, so that to repent really means to re-think or re-assess, which is a much closer interpretation of the word in the original Greek, *metanoia*, which means literally (the use of) a mind beyond the ordinary. Even this does not convey the meaning fully until it is realised that this extraordinary mind is an intelligence of a different order directed by a higher level of consciousness.

Hence metanoia is not something which can be contrived by taking thought but involves the rejection of the incessant clamour of the low mind, which ordinarily demands an entirely disproportionate part of our attention. If one persists in the effort one may be suddenly rewarded with a moment of bliss.

'You have a problem?' said my Angel unexpectedly.

'There is something missing,' I admitted. 'As I understand it this kind of awareness provides much needed food for the soul. Yet any personal advantage is surely entirely secondary to the much more significant nourishment which such endeavours provide for the Astral level. What of the mass of humanity which does not make any conscious effort – and maybe does not even want to?'

'You must distinguish between mechanical and conscious humanity,' he answered. 'The phenomenal world has to be populated with human beings who, as part of organic life, serve the cosmic requirements of that level; but the possibility exists at any given time for a small proportion to play their roles consciously and so provide the required Astral nourishment.'

'Are the rest then of no account?'

'Why this arrogance?' he retorted. 'They have their opportunities in their appropriate time, and may even be responding to conscious influences in ways you know nothing if. What you must concern yourself with is the utilisation of your own opportunities. This is why you are here on earth. Properly directed individual effort can contribute to a higher level of consciousness and thereby increase its availability to others. You must think beyond your conceit.'

I tried to envisage the situation more objectively. One can see that mankind is subject to two kinds of influence, material and spiritual. The former are concerned with contending with the affairs of life and there are many who respond only to these influences, which they manipulate as best they can for their own interests. They regard this, in fact, as the sole purpose of existence and may achieve considerable worldly success. Some even derive their pleasure from causing distress to others, fomenting strife or causing wanton destruction. These we regard as evil, though this is a conditioned judgement. It seems that conflict is part of the cosmic requirement[12] and in the unmanifest world good and evil are complementary aspects of the same pattern. Man's purpose appears to lie not in the elimination of all conflict but in understanding the truth which lies between.

At the same time, there are many people who respond to both types of influence. They make intelligent use of material opportunities but have an (often inarticulate) awareness of spiritual values. They possess a certain inner integrity which they try to maintain even in adversity, being content simply to do what they feel to be right without needing to know why. As Gareth says in Tennyson's *Idylls of the King*, 'Live pure, speak true, right wrong, honour the King. Else wherefore born?'

This simple faith provides the soul with the beginning of the food it needs; and this is not of purely personal benefit because the exercise of faith contributes to the replenishment of the Universe. The mass influence of the faithful, of whatever creed or religion, tends to offset the power of malevolent forces, and so to preserve the necessary balance.

The nourishment, however, can be immeasurably increased in both quantity and quality by the conscious submission to superior direction called metanoia. If this can be practised, the everyday experiences of life acquire new and enriched meanings which begin to supply the soul with real nourishment.

The most significant aspect of this expanded awareness is that it can be exercised simultaneously with the necessary attention to life affairs, which by the very act become material for spiritual development. This is an idea of considerable practical importance for it can transform the quality of the ineluctable pattern of events which has to be played out faithfully in the present recurrence. One can remember that there is a certain (limited) choice in the allocation of the life and the wise soul is not influenced by considerations of material comfort and success, but is concerned with the opportunities for spiritual growth which the events may provide.

There are many difficult or unpleasant situations in life, some of which may appear completely unjust, but it may be that these are exactly what has been asked for at a more conscious level. As an example from my own experience, I was at one time dejected by the collapse of a certain cherished ambition, but this subsequently proved a blessing because it released me from a number of unnecessary requirements.

Indeed, the idea that one has bought one's life is helpful in many situations, particularly in tragic events which may seem at the time to be utterly senseless and unjustified. There was the instance of the young girl who was brutally murdered while on holiday in France, to the great distress of her decent and God-fearing parents, who were concerned less for themselves than for the daughter's soul. One has to see that all the participants in such an event were fulfilling an allotted role from which the individual souls *could* derive significant nourishment.

In general, however, life is a succession of less dramatic events which one takes for granted but which acquire entirely new meaning if one endeavours to participate in them consciously. There is, of course, no compulsion to make any such effort. One can be content to adopt Charles Kingsley's oft-quoted phrase in *Farewell to C.E.G.* – 'Be good sweet maid and let who will be clever.' But this will inevitably prolong the time which has to be spent on earth.

Pondering these ideas in my heart I suddenly perceived that the real purpose of the sojourn on earth is simply the nourishment of the soul. It is a joyous and enduring task, embracing the whole gamut of experience extending far beyond the confines of the time and space of the senses. I saw too that it is a continuing adventure because understanding can never be complete.

I recalled a saying of my old friend and mentor Laurie Goodman that we should learn to live two separate days. This means that while contending with the affairs of life to the best advantage, the situations themselves are really the raw material for spiritual nourishment. Once this is recognised, events can be accepted without objecting or seeking escape, for they are in very truth the 'daily bread' of the familiar prayer, for which we should continually remember to give thanks; and this is the secret of the real endeavour.

Yet it is above all an individual task which cannot be imposed by an external authority, however inspired. Spiritual ideas are essential to awaken the slumbering mind, but they can only serve as directives to an effort which one has to make for oneself; and I recalled how my Angel had consistently refused to supply ready-made answers to my questions but had indicated how I might arrive at these for myself.

We have continually to question what we think we know or understand. Only repeated inquiry by the deeper and more intuitive levels of the mind will induce the Universe to reveal its secrets – and then only grudgingly in exchange for persistent demands. This is the real meaning of prayer, which is not just a hopeful request for assistance but an importunate demand for enlightenment; and it must be not only persistent but based on the certain faith that the answers are already existing in the internal world. As St Thomas Aquinas said many centuries ago,

'Some of the ancients, divining truth yet from far away, reckoned that the soul knows things because it is composed of them.'

Once again I perceived the magnificence of the idea that we do not exist in isolation. The physical bodies which we inhabit necessarily create the illusion of separate individuality but we are actually units in a community of souls in which there is the constant availability of communication and mutual assistance. Whatever the route by which we seek to approach reality, any sincere effort is of value to this spiritual community – and thereby to the Universe. One can envisage a constant interchange of ideas and assistance between souls in various stages of fulfilment of the Grand Design.

References

1 Cerminara, Gina, *Many Mansions* (Neville Spearman, London, 1967).

2 Crookhall, Dr Robert, *The Supreme Adventure* (James Clarke, Cambridge, 1961).

3 Evans-Wentz, W. Y., *The Tibetan Book of the Dead* (Oxford University Press, 1927).

4 Greaves, Helen, *The Wheel of Eternity* (Neville Spearman, London, 1974).

5 Guirdham, A., *The Cathars and Reincarnation* (Neville Spearman, London, 1970).

6 Happold, F. C., *Mysticism* (Chapter 7) (Pelican, London, 1963).

7 Hutton, Bernard, *Healing Hands* (W. H. Allen, London, 1966).

8 Linssen, Robert, *Living Zen* (Allen & Unwin, London, 1958).

9 Lutyens, Mary, *Krishnamurti. The Years of Awakening* (John Murray, London, 1975).

10 Moody, Dr Raymond, *Life after life* (Bantam, New York, 1976).

11 Ouspensky, P. D., *A New Model of the Universe* (Routledge & Kegan Paul, London, 1938).

12 Ouspensky, P. D., *In Search of the Miraculous* (Routledge & Kegan Paul, London, 1965).

13 Nicoll, Maurice, *Living Time* (Watkins, London, 1952).

14 Reyner, J. H., *The Age of Miracles* (Neville Spearman, London, 1975).

15 Reyner, J. H., *The Diary of a Modern Alchemist* (Neville Spearman, London, 1974).

16 Reyner, J. H. with Laurence, G. and Upton, C., *Psionic Medicine* (Routledge & Kegan Paul, London, 1974).

17 Sherwood, Jane, *The Country Beyond* (Neville Spearman, London, 1969).

18 Sherwood, Jane, *Post Mortem Journal* (Neville Spearman, London, 1971).

19 Stewart, J. A., *The Myths of Plato* (Centaur Press, London, 1960).

20 Walker, Benjamin, *Beyond the Body* (Routledge & Kegan Paul, 1974).

Index